A · WEEKEND · PROJECT · BOOK

Tree Houses

YOU · CAN · ACTUALLY · BUILD

A · WEEKEND · PROJECT · BOOK

Tree Houses

YOU · CAN · ACTUALLY · BUILD

David and Jeanie Stiles

Designs and illustrations by David Stiles

HOUGHTON MIFFLIN

BOSTON NEW YORK

For information about permission to reproduce selections from this book, write to Permissions, Houghton Mifflin Company, 215 Park Avenue South, New York, New York 10003.

Library of Congress Cataloging-in-Publication Data
Stiles, David R.
Tree houses you can actually build / David and Jeanie Stiles;
designs and illustrations by David Stiles.
p.   cm. — (A weekend project book)
ISBN 0-395-89273-2
1. Tree houses — Design and construction — Amateurs' manuals.
I. Stiles, Jeanie. II. Title. III. Series: Stiles, David R. Weekend project book series.
TH4885.S75 1998
690'.89 — dc21   98-3511

The information in this book cannot anticipate the individual characteristics of each tree and each tree house. Each builder must accept responsibility for applying the suggestions from this book to a specific location and project, or seek the advice of a competent expert for on-site advice.

Designed by Eugenie S. Delaney

Photography Accessories:
Victoria's Mother, 43 Main Street, East Hampton, NY 11937
Village Toy Shop, 45 Main Street, East Hampton, NY 11937
The Party Shoppe, 82 Park Place, East Hampton, NY 11937

FRONT COVER PHOTO: Cedar-Shingled A-Frame Built on Two Trees
This tree house (see page 68) was built on a hill in the woods within sight of the owners' house. The A-frame roof hinges open on both sides, ventilating the tree house and inviting light to fill the interior. In the winter, the roof can be closed up tight. A lookout porch with a railing was added to the original design. A permanent ladder was attached to the porch, and a handhold was cut into the floor. Spring cleaning became necessary when a raccoon, which had taken up residence over the winter, was spotted peaking out from the side opening. A removable tire swing can be attached to the supporting beams. The shingles have weathered to a soft gray, causing the tree house to blend in with the surrounding oak woods.

Dedicated to Lief Anne, Eben, and Jaime

Acknowledgments

We would like to thank all the tree house owners who let us photograph their tree houses. Although we did not have room to include photographs of each one, every design was wonderful and unique, and they all contributed to the inspiration for this book.

We also would like to thank Ann and John Hulsey, Albert Stiles, Virginia Conklin, and Tim Blenk for their information on trees and tree houses. And thanks to all the kids who modeled for the photographs, helping the tree houses to come alive.

Contents

Introduction

If you think tree houses are just for kids, think again. A tree house represents an escape from family pressures and the demands of society, and it provides a place for children and adults to escape to where no one can phone or reach them.

An increasingly large number of adults are building tree houses as weekend retreats to get away from it all. Before getting out your hammer and saw, however, you might want to consider renting a tree house for a week in St. John, Virgin Islands. A bit more luxurious than camping, vacationing in a tree house can help you gain a different, more uplifting perspective on life and may provide just the incentive you need to build your own.

In the past, tree houses served many different functions. In western New Guinea, a Pygmy tribe lives in a cluster of tree houses, called Khaim, some measuring 40 feet long and 20 feet wide, often perched 60 feet up in massive banyan trees. The people line the slatted walls with bark, thatch the roofs, and reach the tree houses by climbing 3-foot-wide jungle ladders made from tree boughs. An arboreal existence is for them an instant source of cool breezes and a way of escaping from malarial mosquitoes. Tree houses also make perfect hunting perches, and since there is much clan warfare there, the women, children, and elderly can remain safely in the air while the warriors fight below.

Today a tree house is more of a luxury, but nonetheless it is still an escape. More than ever, we need a refuge from the everyday stress of our electronic world. A tree house can be a private place to read, write, paint, or meditate, or it can be a social spot to gather for cocktails or tea for two.

If you own property in the country, plan to build a house there, and are wondering just how to position it, or if you are waiting for a building loan to come through, why not try spending some time in a tree house first? Camp out in your tree house and observe where the sun rises and sets; listen to the sounds of nature and look for the best view. You may decide that you don't really need to build an expensive house after all!

For kids, tree houses are a timeless American tradition. Building a tree house can teach children how to work together with family or friends, how to use tools, and, with luck, how to cultivate good housekeeping skills. Most important, it allows them to be independent and to have a private place of their own where they can escape from grownups and the pressures of everyday life. For a young child, a tree house can be a place to act out fantasies; for a teenager, it can offer privacy and time alone; and for an adult, it can be a creative outlet and a satisfying way to develop carpentry skills.

Most of the tree houses illustrated in this book are purposely made simple so that a child could build them. However, many of the basic building techniques are the same ones used when building larger structures. Since every tree varies in size and shape, it is impossible to provide specific dimensions, but the drawings should give you a good idea of the various construction methods necessary to build your particular tree house. The designs can be changed and embellished according to individual tastes and situations. But the key to building any successful tree house is to maintain an open, airy feeling. You don't want to make the space too confining or enclosed.

It is not always advisable to put a lock on a tree house door. This presents an irresistible challenge to neighborhood kids to try to break in — and they will probably succeed. From a safety point of view, locks also can present a problem if small kids are playing in the house and parents want to be able to check on them from time to time.

Window glass can be hazardous, too, so it is a good idea to eliminate this from your tree house. And actually, it is more in the spirit of tree houses to keep them open, welcoming all visitors (see tear-out sign, page 124). If you simply must have real windows, make them out of unbreakable clear Lexan plastic or Plexiglas, available at most building supply stores.

We have included photographs showing a range of tree houses: very simple designs using platforms; tree houses made from found items only; and elaborate and expensive tree houses with insulation, windows, and a spiral staircase. The only firm rules are that your tree house be fun, inventive, and safe.

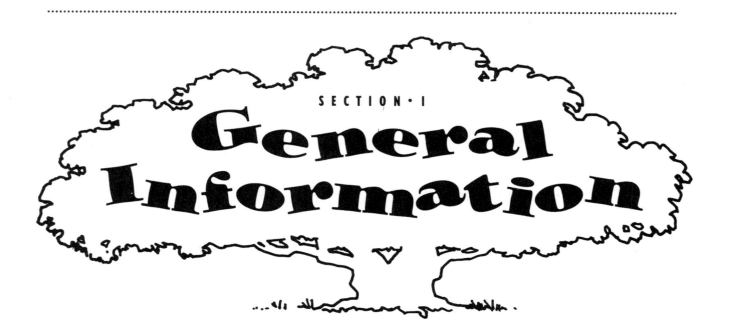

General Information

Where to Build?

If you are thinking about building a tree house in your backyard, be sure to consider your neighbors. Use the grid on page 119 to make a rough sketch and show it to them for their approval. Point out the tree on which you plan to build and ask their advice. (You don't have to follow it.)

Although the look of your tree house is ultimately up to you, your neighbors have good reason to object if you start a tree house with all good intentions but leave it unfinished, affording them a view of awkwardly angled boards silhouetted against the sky. The best solution for all concerned is to situate your tree house so that it is as invisible as possible.

If you have been eyeing the empty lot down the street, be sure you find out who owns it and then get his or her permission before you start your building project. Otherwise, the owner has every right to insist that you tear down your hard work if he or she objects to it.

Perhaps you live near or know of a wooded area and think that no one would care — and possibly never even know — if you built a tree house in some secluded spot there. Be forewarned: somebody always owns the woods, whether it be the federal government, the state, or a private party. Try to find out who owns the land, then ask his or her permission before proceeding with any building plans.

Found Materials

The next big consideration is what to use to build your tree house. The most obvious and economical source of materials is deadwood — logs, branches, and so on — found in the woods. Make sure that the wood you pick is not rotten inside or filled with bugs. Although it's difficult to find long, straight logs in the woods (unless you have unlimited acreage), a tree house made out of logs looks terrific.

Another source of materials is scrap wood

and possibly scrap roofing and building paper from a new house site, which some builders may be willing to give you. Chances are their scrap pile will eventually have to be hauled away to the dump, where they will have to pay a hefty fee to dispose of it, so don't hesitate to inquire about the possibility of helping yourself to their cast-off building materials.

You also might check with your neighbors to see whether they have (or know of someone who has) a shed or other outbuilding that they want to get rid of. You could offer to tear it down for them in return for the wood.

Sometimes lumberyards have quantities of scrap wood that they are throwing out, so inquire there as well. If you have to buy materials, ask at the lumberyard if they have any low-grade lumber suitable for scaffolding. Gray or weathered lumber often gets sold at a cheaper price, and this type of wood will serve your needs perfectly. Whatever type of wood you use, make sure it doesn't have too many knots in any one area, as this may seriously weaken it.

To paint or not to paint — that is up to you. Most tree house builders let their houses weather to look like part of the tree. Some people, however, may want to paint the wood the same color as their home or a forest green to blend in with the woods. Let good taste be your guide.

About Trees

Just about any tree will *do* for building a tree house as long as the tree is healthy and the trunk is a minimum of 6 to 8 inches in diameter. Trees that grow tall and straight, such as southern lodgepole pines, are good for three- or four-legged tree houses, while other sprawling, wide-based trees, such as beech or banyan trees, are more suitable for single-tree construction.

A living tree has heartwood (dead cells), sapwood, medullary rays, cambium, and bark. The sapwood and cambium cells provide and transfer nutrients and water.

Tree Growth

Trees grow in two directions — in circumference and height. Each spring, the sap runs up the outer layer of the tree, just under the bark, sending nutrients to the ends of the branches and into the leaves. As winter approaches, this process stops and then begins again the following spring.

bark

cambium

sapwood

heartwood

Cutting Branches

If you need to cut a branch off a tree, look carefully at the point where it meets the trunk, and you will notice a slight bulge called a collar. This is where you should cut the branch.

If you have a choice, do your pruning when the tree is dormant (summer and winter), since the sap is not running at those times.

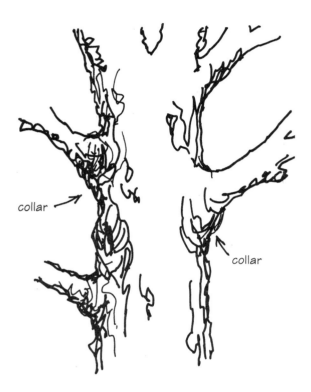

collar

collar

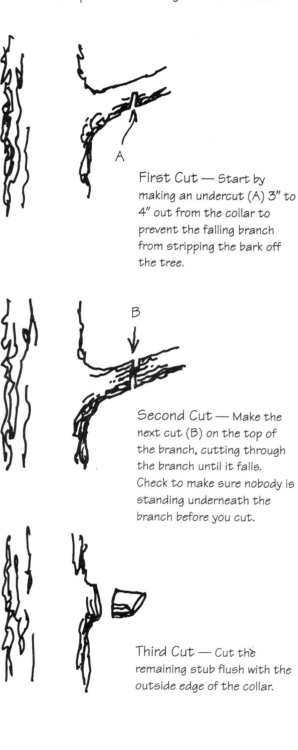

First Cut — Start by making an undercut (A) 3" to 4" out from the collar to prevent the falling branch from stripping the bark off the tree.

Second Cut — Make the next cut (B) on the top of the branch, cutting through the branch until it falls. Check to make sure nobody is standing underneath the branch before you cut.

Third Cut — Cut the remaining stub flush with the outside edge of the collar.

Healing

Resist the temptation to paint the exposed cut with tar or preservative, since a protective callus will form more quickly when the wound is exposed to fresh air. The healing process will begin immediately. You may see some liquid oozing from the wound, which is natural. The tree will gradually grow over the cut, much like a scab forms over a cut on your skin.

Don't do this!

What's wrong with this picture?
(Don't support your ladder on the same
limb that you are cutting.)

**Don't
do this!**

Don't stand under the
limb you are cutting.

Instead

Position yourself above the
branch and behind the tree.

To keep the branch you are
cutting from falling on something
valuable, support it with a rope
tied to a branch above.

Climbing a Tree

Tree climbing, like rock climbing, is a sport in itself. It requires agility, ingenuity, and confidence. Since each tree requires a different approach, it is difficult to describe exactly how to go about it. However, the following general tips should prove helpful.

1. Wear old pants and a shirt with long sleeves to protect your legs and arms from rubbing against the bark and getting chafed.

2. Test each branch before putting your total weight on it.

3. Always make sure that one of your feet and one of your arms is supported by the tree as you move from one branch to another.

4. Don't carry objects into the tree, as this will prevent you from being able to use both hands while climbing. Instead, use a rope to hoist them up.

5. Remember, safety comes first! Concentrate on what you are doing at all times. Don't look down or think about falling — that will only take your mind off your actions!

Injury to Trees

Trees are like us — they can take a lot of punishment before they give up and die. Driving a nail or drilling a lag screw into a tree doesn't help it, but it won't kill the tree either. Trees are more likely to die from lightning, insects, fungus, parasites, lack of water, or severed roots. Although we all want to preserve our trees, our main concern here is to build a safe tree house. Don't be afraid to attach enough screws or nails to make your tree house strong and safe.

If you don't have exactly the right size trees on your property to build a tree house and are lucky enough to live near a wooded area, you can improvise by finding a dead tree and using it for one of the support posts.

ouch

Just make sure that the wood is strong and not filled with rot.

Protect the butt (thicker) end of a log from rot by placing it in a bucket of wood preservative and letting it soak overnight. Then follow the directions for posts on pages 50–51.

Carry it home using two bicycles to support the butt end.

pulley

Use a rope and pulley to hoist it up into position.

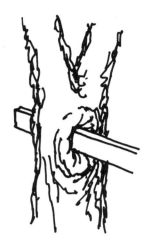

Given time, a tree will grow around anything you attach to it. For example, several years ago we laid a 2x4 in the crotch of a tree branch to install a beam for a swing. Today the beam is permanently embedded, with 6" of new trunk surrounding it.

1st Year

The distance from this height to the ground will remain the same. Only the tops of the trees will get taller.

The width (diameter) of the tree will increase approximately ¼" each year.

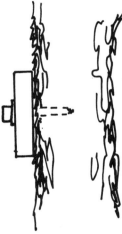

3 Years Later

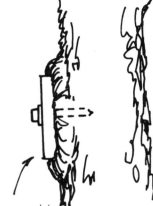

No carpenter could hope to make a joint this tight.

Don't tie a rope or wire tightly around a tree. In a few years, the rope will literally strangle the life out of the tree.

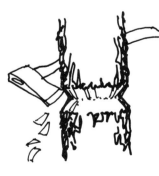

Don't cut the bark around a tree (called girdling), as this will kill the tree.

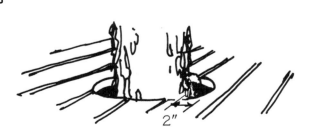

Since a tree trunk grows in diameter, always leave at least 2" of clearance between the tree and the floorboards.

TREE MOVEMENT
and Flexible Joints

Trees will always move in the wind — especially tall, thin trees.
If you are building in a windy area, or if your trees are likely to sway and bend,
build your tree house with flexible joints (see also page 46).

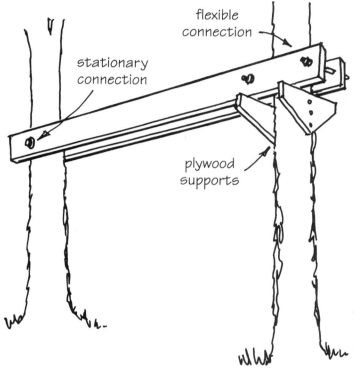

flexible connection

stationary connection

plywood supports

Note: We have found that when a beam is attached to two trees, one end of the beam will become permanently attached to one tree, and the other end will remain loose, allowing the trees to be independent of each other in the wind.

Beams rest on plywood triangle supports and are loosely held in place by two ½"-dia. threaded rods which can be loosened each year to allow for tree growth.

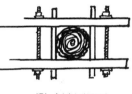

PLAN VIEW

FLEXIBLE ROPE CONNECTION

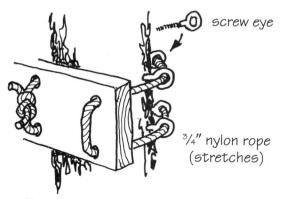

screw eye

¾" nylon rope (stretches)

Check rope every year for chafing.
Screw eyes keep the rope from chafing the tree.

FLEXIBLE SLOT CONNECTION

1"x2" slots

½"-dia. lag screws with oversize washers loosely fitted so beam can shift in the wind.

LUMBER

If you decide to buy new lumber for your tree house, here is a guide to help you.

Nail two 2x8s together to make a 3"-thick
beam that can span up to 14'.

Used for extra-heavy
beam spans up to 8'.

Used for heavy braces and
crossbeams and spans up to 6'.

Used for short braces
and spans up to 4'.

Used for flooring.

Used for
cleats.

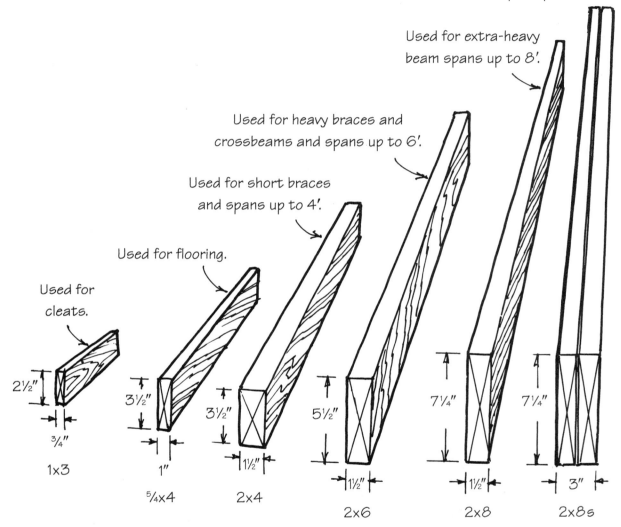

2½"   ¾"   1x3

3½"   1"   ⁵⁄₄x4

3½"   1½"   2x4

5½"   1½"   2x6

7¼"   1½"   2x8

7¼"   3"   2x8s

Pressure-Treated Lumber

Pressure-treated (P.T.) lumber will generally last 20 to 30 years.
If you choose to use it when building your tree house, make sure to take adequate precautions.
Don't breathe in the sawdust or burn the scrap wood. Wear gloves when working
with P.T. lumber and always wash your hands after handling it.

HAND TOOLS

Here are some of the tools you will need to build a tree house.

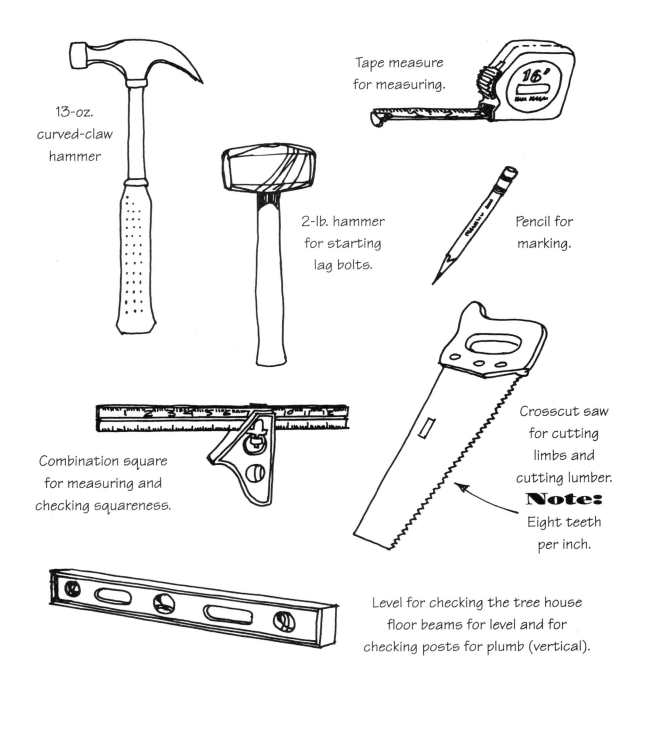

13-oz.
curved-claw
hammer

Tape measure
for measuring.

2-lb. hammer
for starting
lag bolts.

Pencil for
marking.

Combination square
for measuring and
checking squareness.

Crosscut saw
for cutting
limbs and
cutting lumber.
Note:
Eight teeth
per inch.

Level for checking the tree house
floor beams for level and for
checking posts for plumb (vertical).

HAND TOOLS continued

Choose one of three types of wrenches.

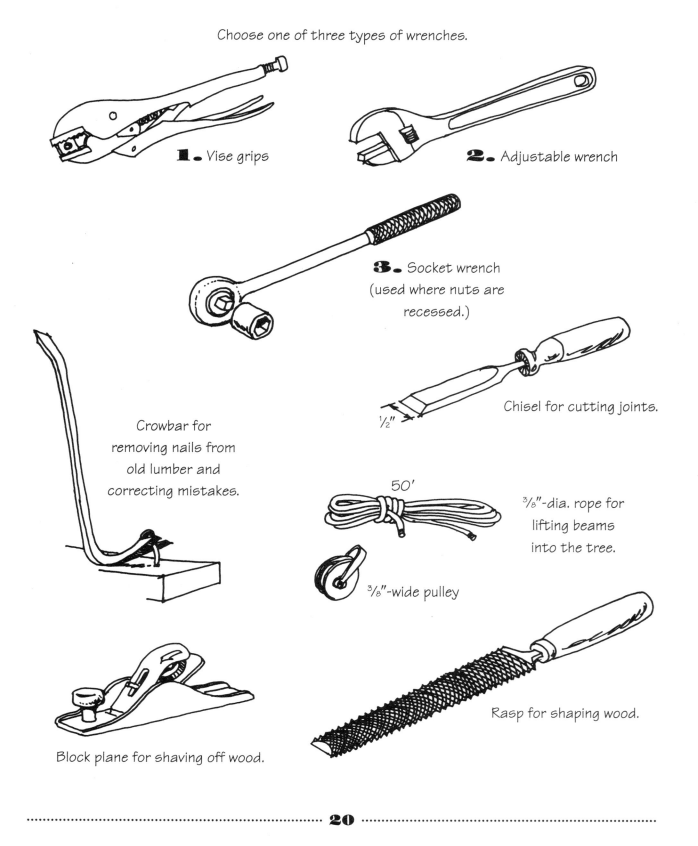

1. Vise grips

2. Adjustable wrench

3. Socket wrench (used where nuts are recessed.)

Chisel for cutting joints.

½"

Crowbar for removing nails from old lumber and correcting mistakes.

50'

⅜"-dia. rope for lifting beams into the tree.

⅜"-wide pulley

Block plane for shaving off wood.

Rasp for shaping wood.

POWER TOOLS

These tools make the job easier.

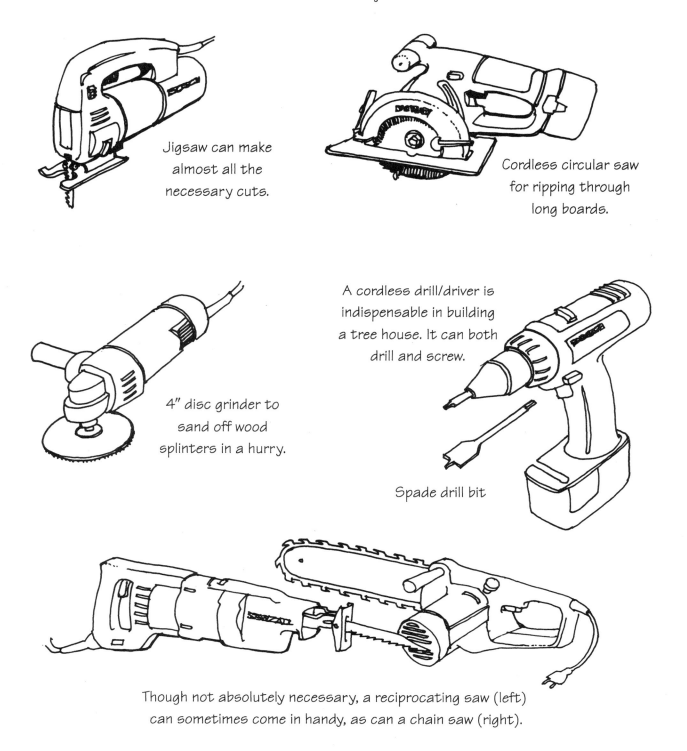

Jigsaw can make almost all the necessary cuts.

Cordless circular saw for ripping through long boards.

4" disc grinder to sand off wood splinters in a hurry.

A cordless drill/driver is indispensable in building a tree house. It can both drill and screw.

Spade drill bit

Though not absolutely necessary, a reciprocating saw (left) can sometimes come in handy, as can a chain saw (right).

NAILS, BOLTS & SCREWS

These are some of the most useful nails, bolts, and screws.
Make sure they are galvanized (coated) to keep them from rusting.

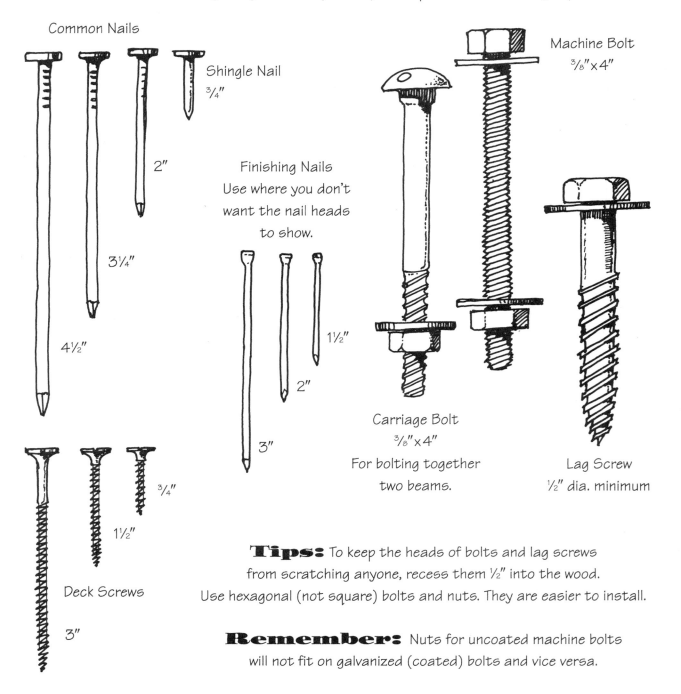

Common Nails

Shingle Nail
3/4"

2"

3 1/4"

4 1/2"

Finishing Nails
Use where you don't
want the nail heads
to show.

1 1/2"

2"

3"

Deck Screws

3/4"

1 1/2"

3"

Machine Bolt
3/8" x 4"

Carriage Bolt
3/8" x 4"
For bolting together
two beams.

Lag Screw
1/2" dia. minimum

Tips: To keep the heads of bolts and lag screws
from scratching anyone, recess them 1/2" into the wood.
Use hexagonal (not square) bolts and nuts. They are easier to install.

Remember: Nuts for uncoated machine bolts
will not fit on galvanized (coated) bolts and vice versa.

SCREWS & PILOT HOLES

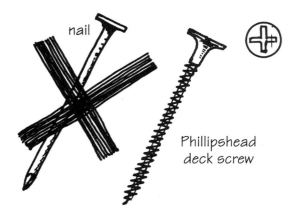

nail

Phillipshead
deck screw

Important: We recommend using galvanized deck screws instead of nails when building a tree house. Screws not only hold better, but they also can be removed. It almost always becomes necessary at one time or another to remove and reposition beams as you build a tree house. Screws also make it easier to remove the tree house if and when it no longer serves a purpose.

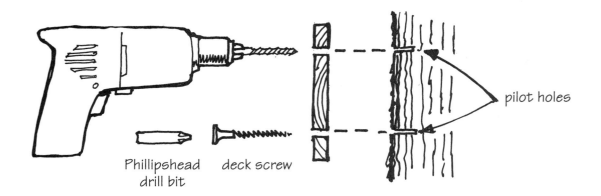

Phillipshead
drill bit

deck screw

pilot holes

Before installing screws, always drill a pilot hole — slightly larger in diameter than the screw itself — in the wood that you are screwing to the tree. If possible, have two drills handy — one for drilling the pilot hole and one for drilling the screw through the beam and into the tree. If drilling a screw into a tree becomes difficult, remove the screw and drill an **undersize** pilot hole in the tree, or coat the screw with soap and try again.

Note: There should be at least 2″ of screw thread embedded in the tree if it is a hardwood and 3″ if it is a softwood.

NAILING

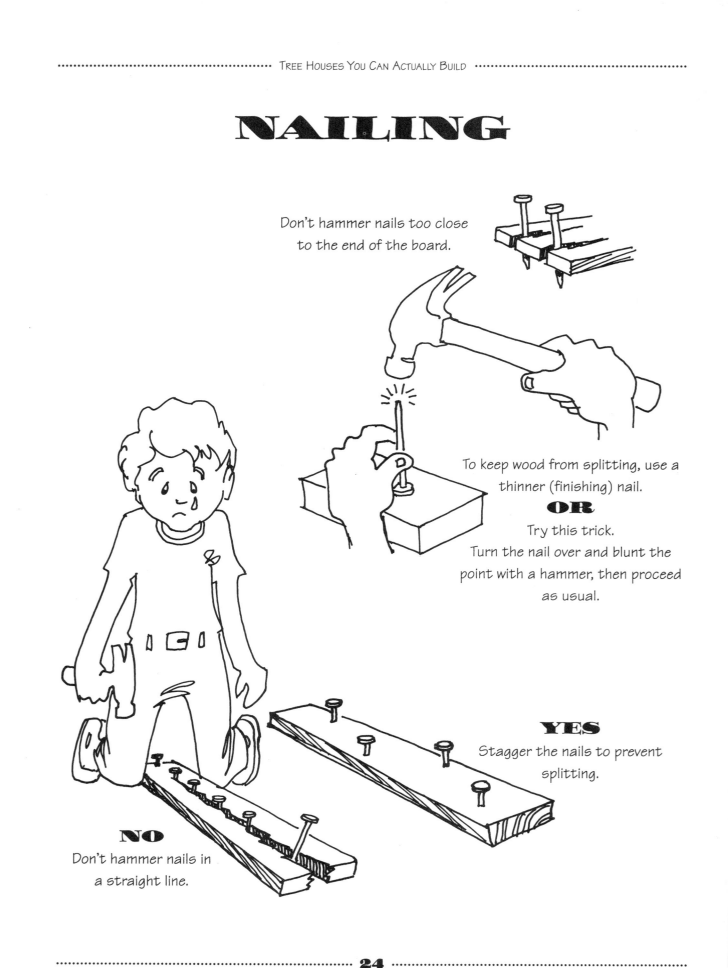

Don't hammer nails too close to the end of the board.

To keep wood from splitting, use a thinner (finishing) nail.

OR

Try this trick.
Turn the nail over and blunt the point with a hammer, then proceed as usual.

YES

Stagger the nails to prevent splitting.

NO

Don't hammer nails in a straight line.

TOENAILING
Beams to Branches

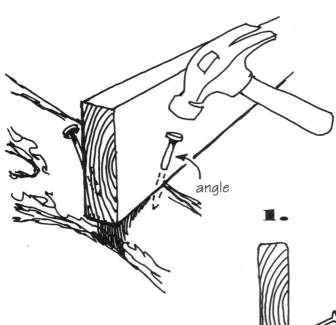

angle

Hint:
Bent nails are actually better
for this particular job.
OR
Try starting the nail at an angle,
bend it down, and finish nailing.

1.   **2.**   **3.**

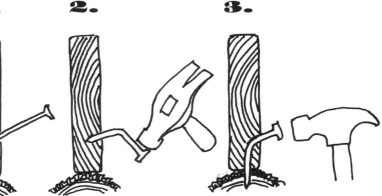

When the place you want to
nail is out of reach, wedge a
nail into the claws of the
hammer and start the nail
with one blow while holding
on to a support with your
other hand.

Before trying to nail a board up into a tree,
start the nails on the ground so that the
points are sticking out the other side.

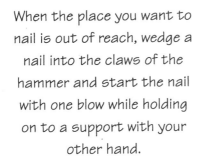

Hold the nail head in
place with chewing gum.

Then climb the tree and nail it on.

How to Install
LAG SCREWS

Use lag screws that are at least ½" in diameter. Thinner ones can break off under stress caused by tree movement or growth.

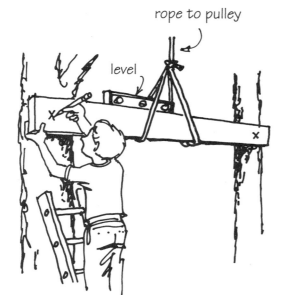

rope to pulley

level

Using a rope and pulley, hoist the beam into position and check to make sure it is level. Mark where the beam touches the tree.

Drill a ½"-diameter hole through each end of the beam.

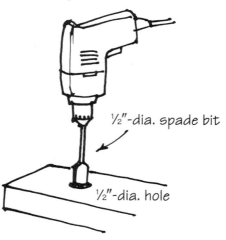

½"-dia. spade bit

½"-dia. hole

Hammer the lag screw into the tree with several hard blows, then, with a wrench, turn the screw a quarter turn only. Pound the screw head again, very hard, and make another quarter turn. Do this about six more times to make sure the screw threads are securely caught in the wood fibers of the tree. Continue screwing until the washer depresses into the beam.

ROPES & KNOTS

It is very helpful to have a rope attached to a pulley to help you hoist beams into the tree while you are framing the floor. To do this, choose a branch high in the tree that is directly over the point where you will be working and use an extension ladder (you can rent one). Or you can tie a heaving knot (see page 29) in one end of the rope and throw it over a limb, or attach a pear-shaped bag filled with pebbles to the end of a rope and throw the rope over a limb.

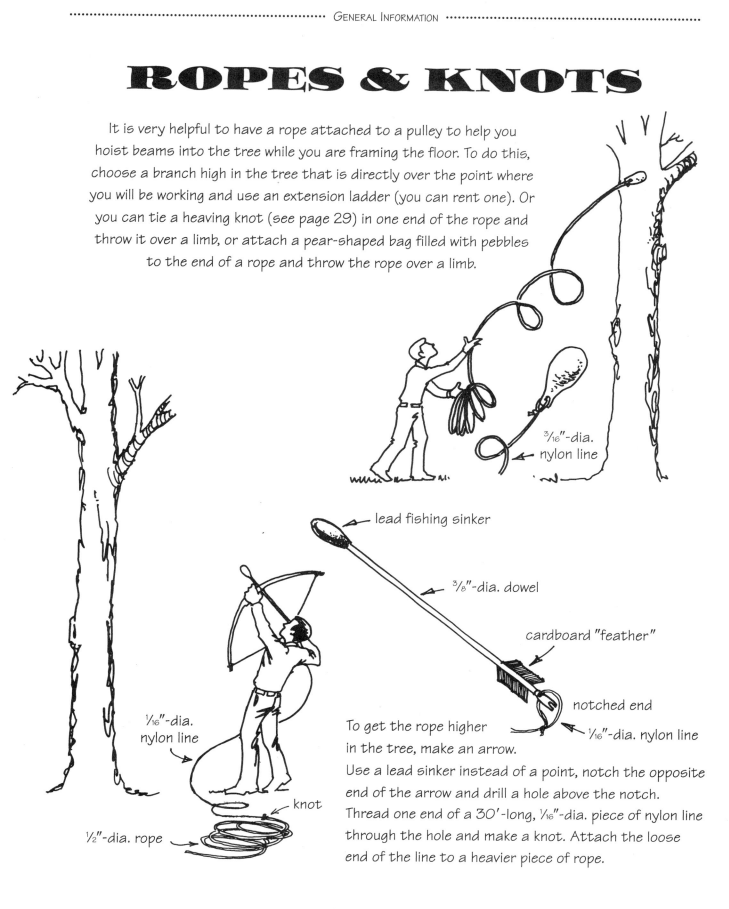

3/16"-dia. nylon line

lead fishing sinker

3/8"-dia. dowel

cardboard "feather"

notched end

1/16"-dia. nylon line

1/16"-dia. nylon line

1/2"-dia. rope

knot

To get the rope higher in the tree, make an arrow. Use a lead sinker instead of a point, notch the opposite end of the arrow and drill a hole above the notch. Thread one end of a 30'-long, 1/16"-dia. piece of nylon line through the hole and make a knot. Attach the loose end of the line to a heavier piece of rope.

Once you have the rope over a branch high in the tree, make a bowline knot (see page 29) in one end of the rope and attach a pulley, with its own rope included, to the loop. Feed the end of the rope you are holding through the loop and raise the pulley to the tree branch. From then on, you can use the pulley to hoist materials into the tree.

Types of
ROPES & KNOTS

Rope comes in several varieties — hemp, manila, polypropylene, Dacron, and nylon. **Never** use polypropylene (yellow) rope, as it will fray and deteriorate in the sun. Instead, we recommend using nylon rope, which stretches and is rot resistant.

 The FIGURE EIGHT or STOP KNOT can be used to stop the line from running through a pulley.

 The SLIP KNOT tightens as it is pulled around an object.

The SQUARE KNOT is used to bind two objects together.

The CLOVE HITCH is used to hang an object from a horizontal branch or beam.

The BOWLINE is a sailor's most reliable knot.

Cross in back.   tight part

Loop over twice.

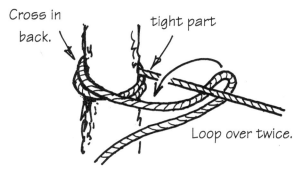

The HALF HITCH

To tie a rope temporarily to a tree, wrap the rope around the tree twice and tie two half hitches around the tight part.

The HEAVING KNOT is used for throwing a rope over a branch.

ROPE LASHING

Use ½"-dia. nylon rope, which stretches and is rot resistant.
To be safe, however, remember to check it every two or three years.
Rope strength 7,000 lbs.

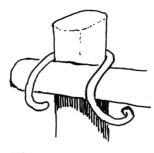 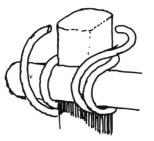 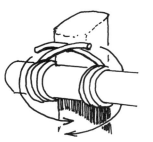 

1. Loop over.

2. Cross in back.

3. Make frapping turns around the lashing to tighten the rope.

4. Finish the lashing with a square knot.

STEPS WARNING!

Do NOT make steps like these.

Very dangerous!

See the next page for ways to make SAFE steps.

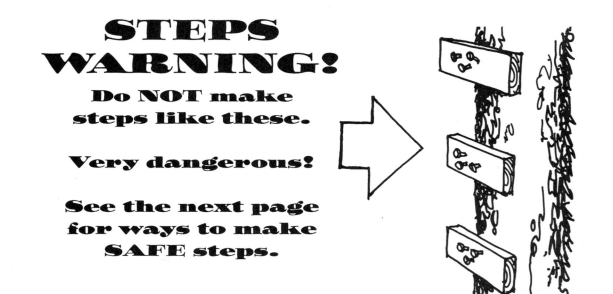

STEPS

STEPS should be checked regularly each year and tested by tying a rope to the step and pulling down hard while standing on the ground.

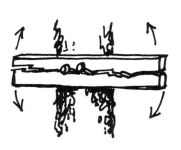

One-board steps are BAD because the step can either pivot or pull out.

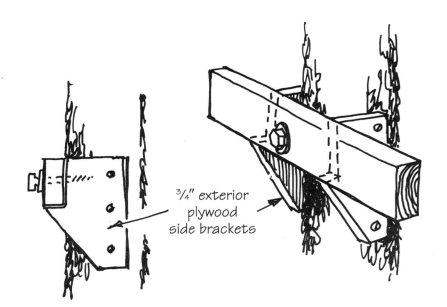

A better way to make steps is to cut up exterior plywood sheathing (often available in scrap piles where new houses are being built). Cut the plywood into side brackets, as shown here, and nail them to the tree. The step rests in the notch and is screwed into the tree with a heavy lag screw.

¾" exterior plywood side brackets

STEPS continued

Here are some variations.

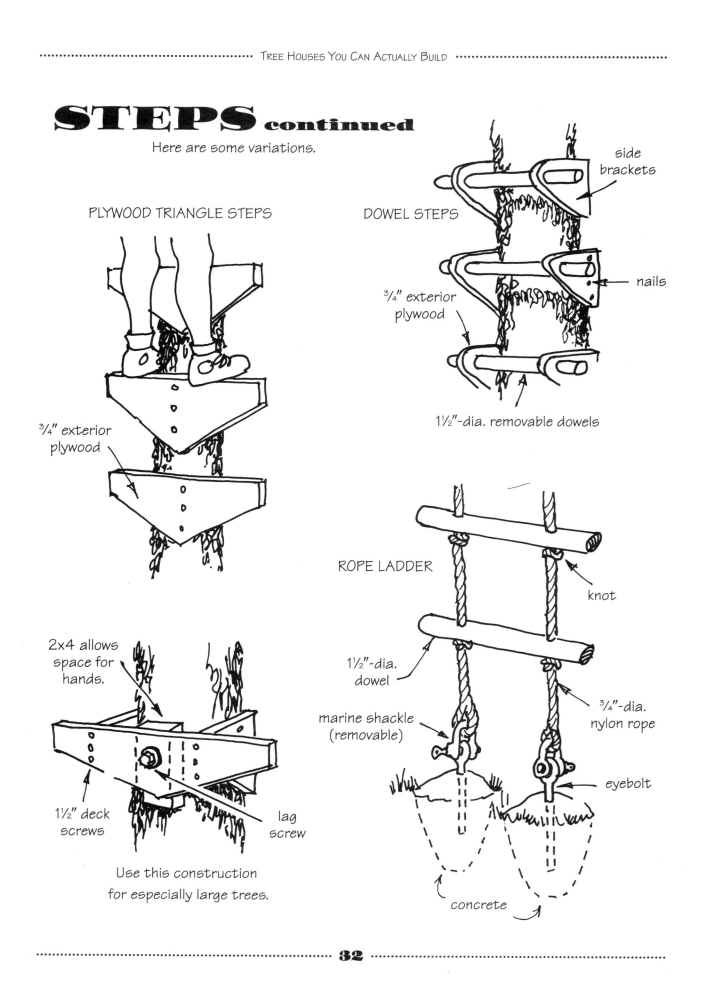

PLYWOOD TRIANGLE STEPS

¾" exterior plywood

DOWEL STEPS

side brackets

nails

¾" exterior plywood

1½"-dia. removable dowels

ROPE LADDER

knot

1½"-dia. dowel

marine shackle (removable)

¾"-dia. nylon rope

eyebolt

concrete

2x4 allows space for hands.

1½" deck screws

lag screw

Use this construction for especially large trees.

MORE STEPS

TELEPHONE POLE STEPS
Good for **small** trees only.

Predrill a hole and screw a ½"-dia. lag screw into the tree.

3½"

2x4 STEP
Good for **large** trees.

½"x5" lag screw

2x4

nail

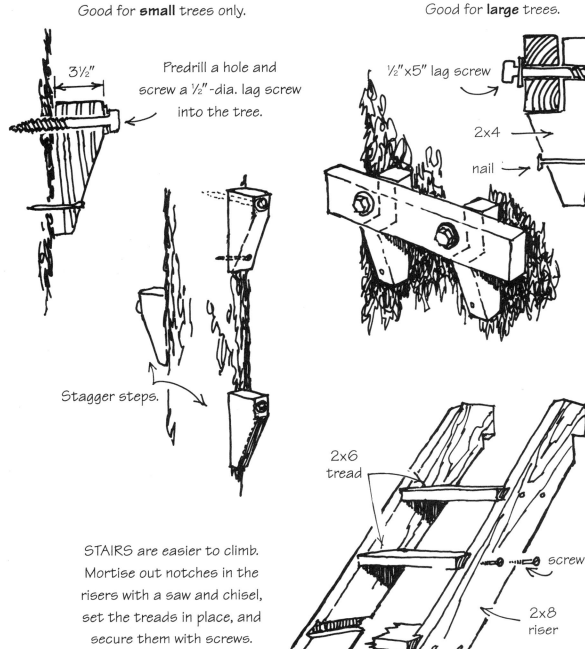

Stagger steps.

STAIRS are easier to climb. Mortise out notches in the risers with a saw and chisel, set the treads in place, and secure them with screws.

2x6 tread

screw

2x8 riser

HANDMADE LADDERS

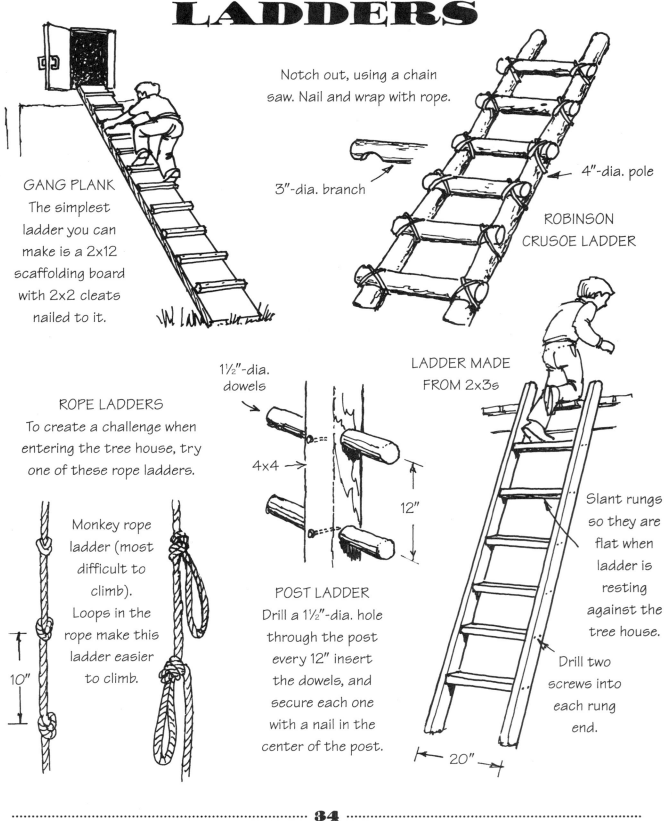

Notch out, using a chain saw. Nail and wrap with rope.

GANG PLANK
The simplest ladder you can make is a 2x12 scaffolding board with 2x2 cleats nailed to it.

3"-dia. branch

4"-dia. pole

ROBINSON CRUSOE LADDER

1½"-dia. dowels

LADDER MADE FROM 2x3s

ROPE LADDERS
To create a challenge when entering the tree house, try one of these rope ladders.

4x4

12"

Monkey rope ladder (most difficult to climb). Loops in the rope make this ladder easier to climb.

10"

POST LADDER
Drill a 1½"-dia. hole through the post every 12" insert the dowels, and secure each one with a nail in the center of the post.

Slant rungs so they are flat when ladder is resting against the tree house.

Drill two screws into each rung end.

20"

LADDER SAFETY

Although ladders are indispensable when building a tree house, they can be dangerous. Here are some things to watch out for.

Make sure your ladder is stable.
If the ground is not level, either put a flat board under the short leg or dig a hole for the long leg.

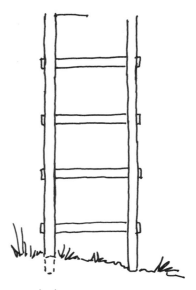

hole

Never put your total weight on a ladder above the fulcrum point, as this could flip the bottom of the ladder out and cause you to fall.

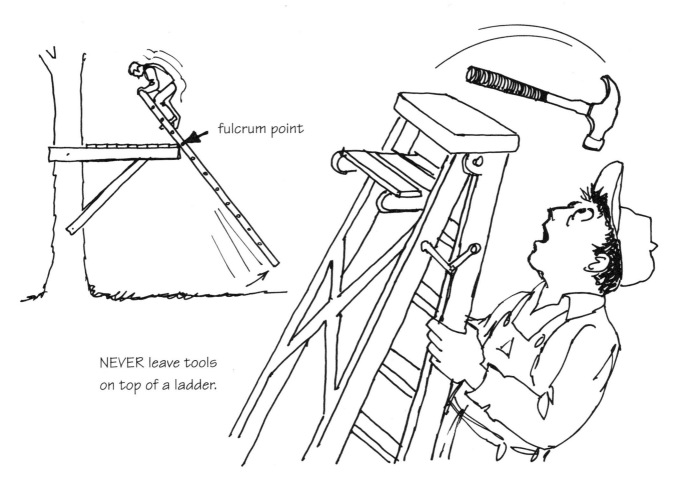

fulcrum point

NEVER leave tools on top of a ladder.

HANDLES

A strategically placed handle is a welcome sight for a tree house climber. Make sure they are well fastened by testing them each year.

Handholds cut in floor.

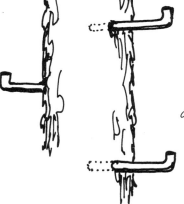

½"x10" steel anchor bars (similar to telephone pole handles) can be drilled into a tree and used for steps.

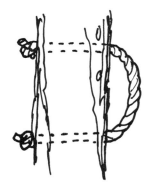

A rope handle can be made from a piece of ¾"-dia. nylon rope, knotted on the back of the tree or post.

A mason's wood float can double as a convenient handle.

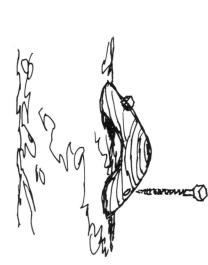

A crooked branch found in the woods can be cut to make a natural-looking handle. Use ⅜"x4" lag screws to fasten it to the tree.

A shed handle or a 2x4 holder bracket can serve as a handle.

SAFETY ALOFT

Safety is the major consideration when building a tree house. Before beginning any task, always consider your safety first. Here are some useful tips to keep in mind.

1. Decide on your climbing route before beginning.

2. When climbing in a tree, always make sure you have an accessible limb or rope to grab onto in case you lose your balance.

3. Keep your hands free for climbing by carrying your tools, nails, and bolts in a cloth nail bag (available free at many lumberyards).

4. Saw off any dead branches that could break.

5. Rig a rope and pulley high in the tree to hold beams in place while you install them (see page 28).

6. Check the tree house each year for rot and weak or loose boards.

7. Provide a soft ground cover below the tree house to soften a fall.

8. Remove any rusted nails and sand any wood that might cause splinters.

9. Avoid building unnecessarily high in a tree.

10. Brace your tree platform to make it extra strong (see page 49).

11. Provide strong handles where needed (for instance, at the top of ladders and inside doorways).

12. Check periodically to make sure rope is sound and not rotten, frayed, or unbraided.

13. Make sure your ladder is level and stable each time you move it.

14. Make sure that an extension ladder is facing in the correct direction.

15. Make sure the rope of a safety harness is resting in the crotch of a strong branch.

SAFETY ALOFT continued

Be careful when removing nails from trees.
Always keep one arm around something stationary
and use a rope safety harness (see page 39).

To Remove Nails

Use a wrecking bar or crowbar
for more leverage.

If you don't have a wrecking bar,
use a block under the hammer
head to remove stubborn nails.

SAFETY HARNESS

When using a safety harness, make sure that the rope from the safety harness is
resting in the crotch of a strong branch so that your support is not based on your own weight.
By relieving the strain on the rope, the harness can be moved up and
down the tree without removing the knot.

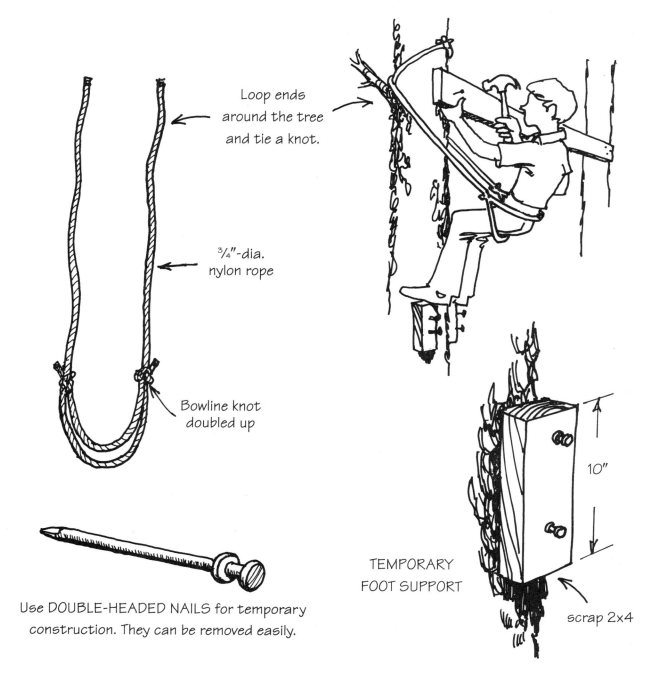

Loop ends
around the tree
and tie a knot.

¾"-dia.
nylon rope

Bowline knot
doubled up

Use DOUBLE-HEADED NAILS for temporary
construction. They can be removed easily.

TEMPORARY
FOOT SUPPORT

10"

scrap 2x4

FIRST AID

Make this small first aid kit from a soap dish and stock it with these items.

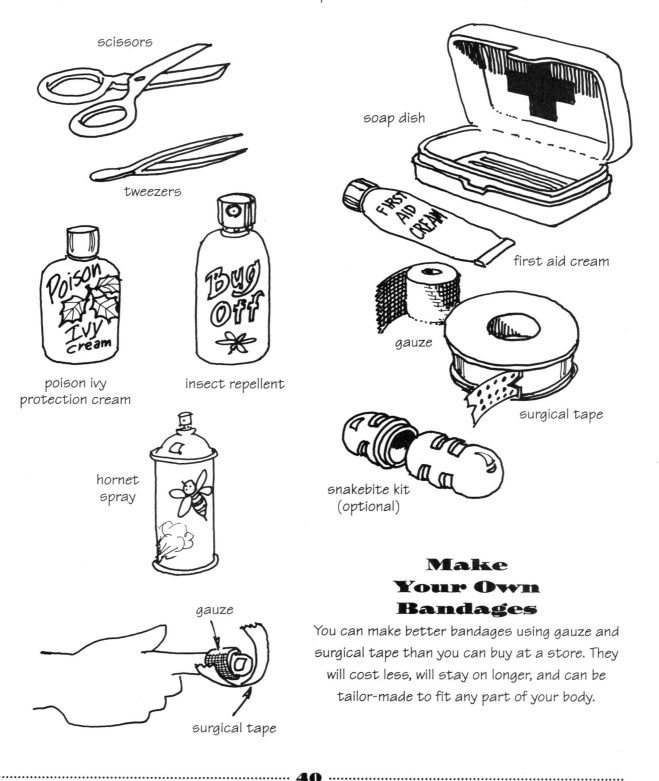

scissors

tweezers

soap dish

first aid cream

poison ivy
protection cream

insect repellent

gauze

surgical tape

hornet
spray

snakebite kit
(optional)

gauze

surgical tape

Make Your Own Bandages

You can make better bandages using gauze and surgical tape than you can buy at a store. They will cost less, will stay on longer, and can be tailor-made to fit any part of your body.

Tree House Basics

Two Approaches to Building a Tree House

The first approach is to hoist a bunch of boards into a very large tree and start nailing or screwing them to the tree wherever there are two branches at the same level. This approach requires no specific plan at all; rather, it uses the tree to suggest the design of the structure. It is a very spontaneous, creative way to build a tree house. Its main challenge is finding a way to build a **level** platform. Ways of dealing with this and other problems that confront the freeform tree house builder are detailed in the next few pages. If you are an inventive person who likes to dive into a project and deal with issues as they arise, this is the method for you.

The second approach is for those who like to know what they are doing before they begin. It takes into consideration the typical situations that you are most likely to find: one tree to build in, two trees to build in, three trees to build in, and four trees to build in. In each case, we provide a specific design that you can follow in step-by-step fashion according to the number and grouping of trees available to you. These four plus another basic design are described in Section III (see pages 60–92).

Choosing the Right Tree

Begin by studying the trees available to you. Walk around them and scrutinize them carefully from all angles while taking into account these four considerations.

1. IS THE TREE STRONG ENOUGH TO SUPPORT A TREE HOUSE? If you are using only one tree, the tree should be at least 1 foot in diameter at the base. If you are using several trees, they should be at least 6 to 8 inches in diameter.

2. IS THE TREE DEAD, or are there any dead branches that might fall down in a windstorm and damage the tree house? It is easy to identify dead trees in the summer due to their lack of green leaves. In the winter, look for buds on the ends of a tree's branches as a sign that it is alive.

3. DISTANCE FROM A HOUSE is an important consideration if you are planning to use electric tools. If the tree you choose is too far for an electric extension cord, you can predrill some of the large holes before carrying your lumber to the tree. If this is not feasible, you can rent or buy a cordless (battery-operated) drill.

4. HOW HIGH FROM THE GROUND SHOULD A TREE HOUSE BE? Before you build your tree house in the top of the tallest tree, bear in mind that the greatest chance of falling out of a tree house occurs when you are building it. It is impossible to hold a hammer in one hand, hold a board in another, hold a nail in a third, and hold on to the tree with a fourth. The answer is to build close enough to the ground so that you can reach the platform while standing on the ground. You will get a lofty feeling of euphoria even when perched only 6 feet in the air.

Look for a strong, live tree with thick branches within easy reach from the ground.

PLANNING
a Tree House in Your Mind

While looking at a tree, pretend that your arms are branches holding a large box. Then try to imagine which branches in the tree a large box would rest on and build your tree house there.

THE PLATFORM

The most important part of building a tree house is erecting a strong, level platform in the tree. Once this is done, the rest goes quite easily.

To determine where to build a platform, connect several points in the tree with mason's string. Use a line level and temporary blocks or supports to make the strings level.

Tree houses don't have to be square, but they must be LEVEL.

Another way to determine where connection points might be in the tree is to tape a 2' level to a long, straight board and hold it up to the tree.

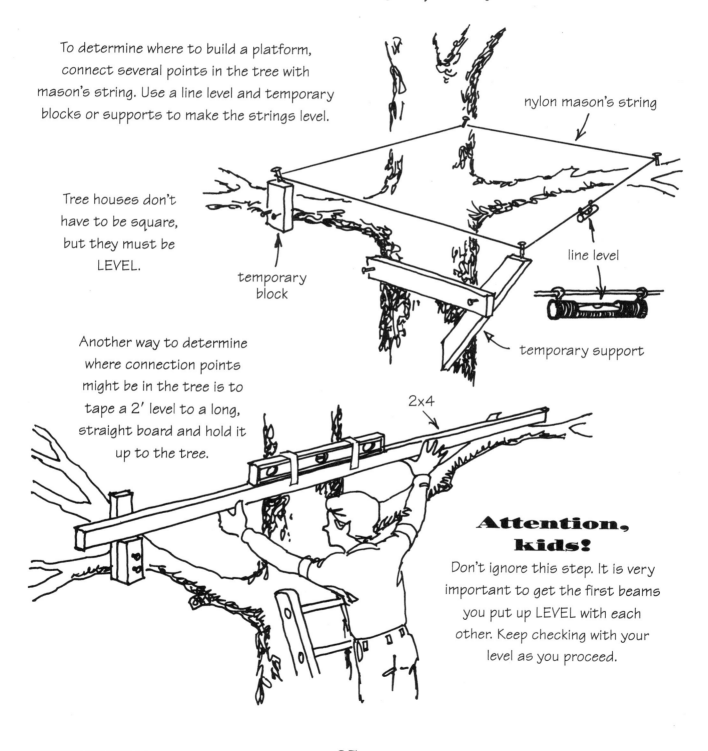

nylon mason's string

temporary block

line level

temporary support

2x4

Attention, kids!

Don't ignore this step. It is very important to get the first beams you put up LEVEL with each other. Keep checking with your level as you proceed.

How to Make the Platform Level

Construct special supports on which the platform beams will rest.
(For the length and size of beams, refer to page 18.) You will need at least three level points
on which to rest the tree house platform. One of these points might be the tree trunk itself.
The others might have to be built up from the branches, as shown here.

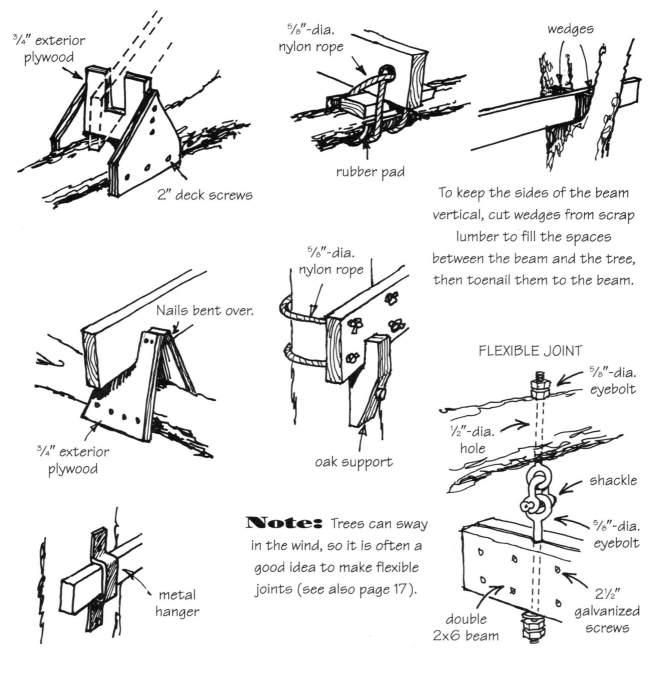

¾" exterior plywood

2" deck screws

⅝"-dia. nylon rope

rubber pad

wedges

To keep the sides of the beam vertical, cut wedges from scrap lumber to fill the spaces between the beam and the tree, then toenail them to the beam.

Nails bent over.

¾" exterior plywood

⅝"-dia. nylon rope

oak support

FLEXIBLE JOINT

⅝"-dia. eyebolt

½"-dia. hole

shackle

⅝"-dia. eyebolt

2½" galvanized screws

double 2x6 beam

metal hanger

Note: Trees can sway in the wind, so it is often a good idea to make flexible joints (see also page 17).

Some Tips on
FRAMING THE PLATFORM

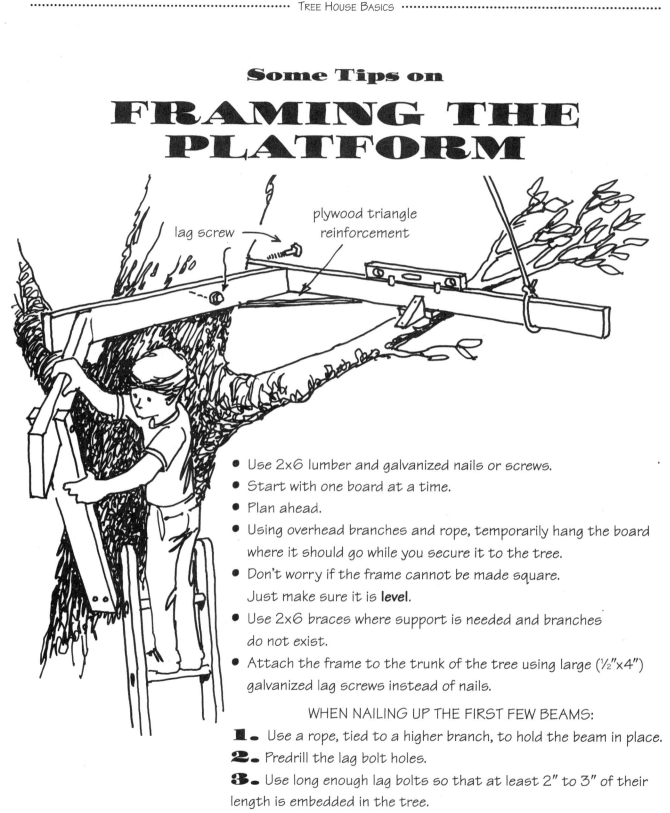

lag screw

plywood triangle reinforcement

- Use 2x6 lumber and galvanized nails or screws.
- Start with one board at a time.
- Plan ahead.
- Using overhead branches and rope, temporarily hang the board where it should go while you secure it to the tree.
- Don't worry if the frame cannot be made square. Just make sure it is **level**.
- Use 2x6 braces where support is needed and branches do not exist.
- Attach the frame to the trunk of the tree using large (½"x4") galvanized lag screws instead of nails.

WHEN NAILING UP THE FIRST FEW BEAMS:

1. Use a rope, tied to a higher branch, to hold the beam in place.

2. Predrill the lag bolt holes.

3. Use long enough lag bolts so that at least 2" to 3" of their length is embedded in the tree.

4. Predrill the hole for a 3½" screw, which is used to position the beam. Use a reversible drill to reposition it until it is level.

- Keep joints flexible so that they move with the tree when the wind blows (see illustration).
- Use 2x4s spaced every 16" for floor joists and cover them with ⁵⁄₄x6 decking spaced ¼" apart or ¾" exterior plywood.
- Once the platform is finished, proceed as shown in Section III (see pages 60–92).

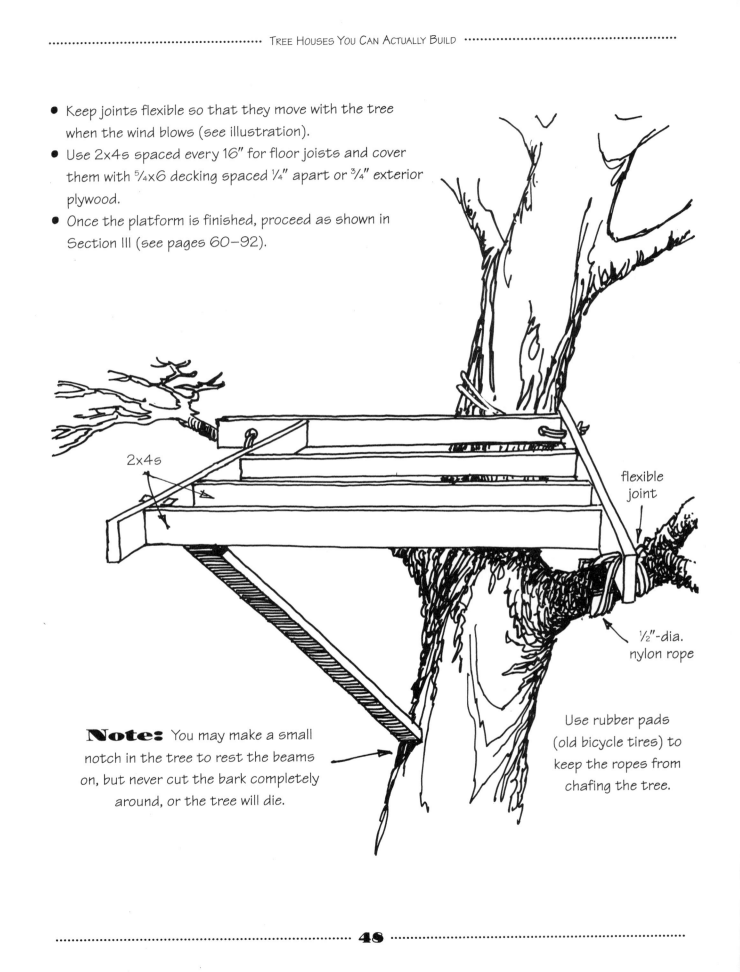

2x4s

flexible joint

½"-dia. nylon rope

Note: You may make a small notch in the tree to rest the beams on, but never cut the bark completely around, or the tree will die.

Use rubber pads (old bicycle tires) to keep the ropes from chafing the tree.

DIAGONAL BRACES

The best way to strengthen a tree house is to
use diagonal braces to support the beams.

When the beam and brace are aligned over each other, notch the
beam (using a jigsaw) and screw the brace to the beam.

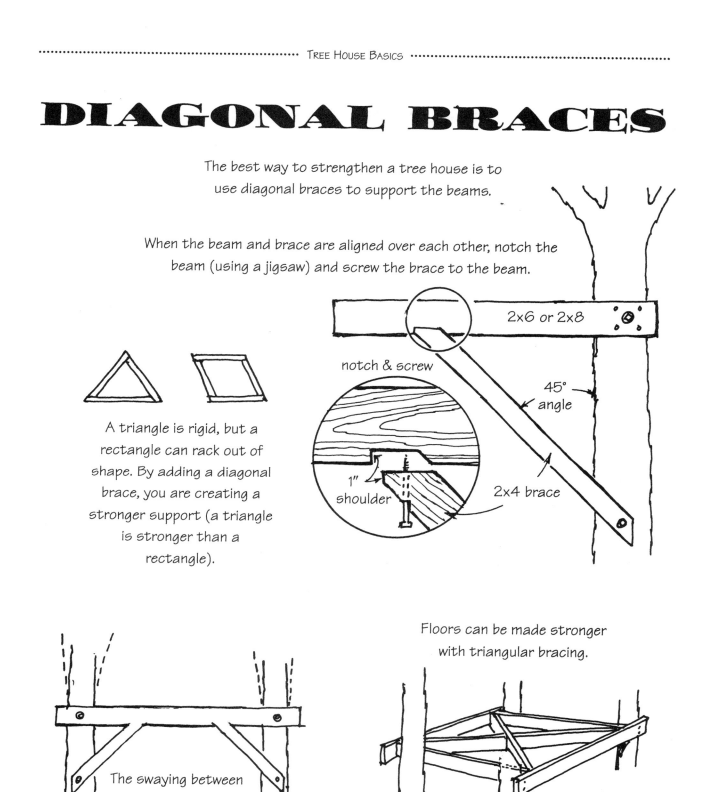

2x6 or 2x8

notch & screw

45°
angle

A triangle is rigid, but a
rectangle can rack out of
shape. By adding a diagonal
brace, you are creating a
stronger support (a triangle
is stronger than a
rectangle).

1"
shoulder

2x4 brace

The swaying between
trees can be greatly
reduced by using
braces.

Floors can be made stronger
with triangular bracing.

Cut notches in
center where
pieces intersect.

POSTS

If you plan on using posts to build your tree house, here are some useful tips.

Almost any post partially buried in the ground is not likely to last long unless protected from DRY ROT and TERMITES. This is nature's way of returning organic matter to its original state, providing nourishment for new plants. It is up to you to take measures to stop this natural transition. Otherwise, your posts may be reduced to a pulpy mush in less than a year.

The best precaution is to use a rot-resistant wood that does not appeal to termites and other wood borers. These woods are, in order of preference, locust, redwood, cypress, and cedar. Unless you are lucky enough to find locust, you will probably have to settle for 4x4 construction-type redwood, which should outlast at least one generation of children. Inspect the posts before buying them to make sure there are not too many knots in one area.

Another alternative is pressure-treated (P.T.) posts, which should last approximately 30 years.

Here are some additional precautions you can take to help ensure that your tree house will still be around for your grandchildren to enjoy.

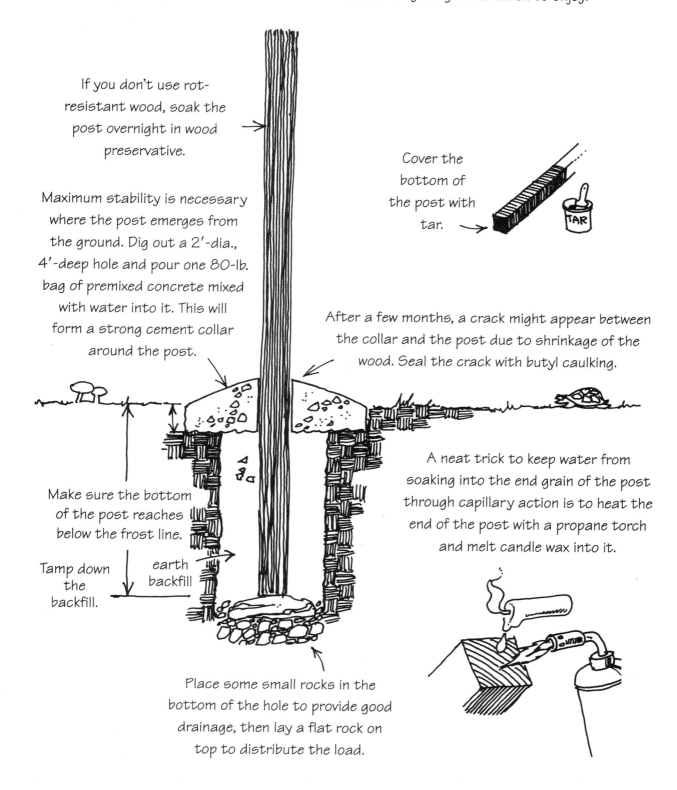

If you don't use rot-resistant wood, soak the post overnight in wood preservative.

Maximum stability is necessary where the post emerges from the ground. Dig out a 2'-dia., 4'-deep hole and pour one 80-lb. bag of premixed concrete mixed with water into it. This will form a strong cement collar around the post.

Cover the bottom of the post with tar.

After a few months, a crack might appear between the collar and the post due to shrinkage of the wood. Seal the crack with butyl caulking.

Make sure the bottom of the post reaches below the frost line.

Tamp down the backfill.

earth backfill

A neat trick to keep water from soaking into the end grain of the post through capillary action is to heat the end of the post with a propane torch and melt candle wax into it.

Place some small rocks in the bottom of the hole to provide good drainage, then lay a flat rock on top to distribute the load.

CONSTRUCTION TIPS

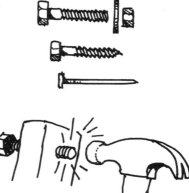

- When deciding what type of fastener to use, remember that a screw is twice as strong as a nail, and a bolt is twice as strong as a screw.

- Never pound the end of a bolt with a metal hammer when removing it from a hole, as this may damage the threads, rendering it useless.

- It is safer to use two 2x4s nailed together than one 4x4. A single piece of lumber may have a weak spot in it, but it is unlikely that two boards will both have a weak spot in the same place.

- Position beams so that there are no knots on the underside, as this can cause the boards to split.

Bad   Better

- To make the connection between a beam and the tree, cut wedges using a hammer and chisel and glue them in place with construction adhesive.

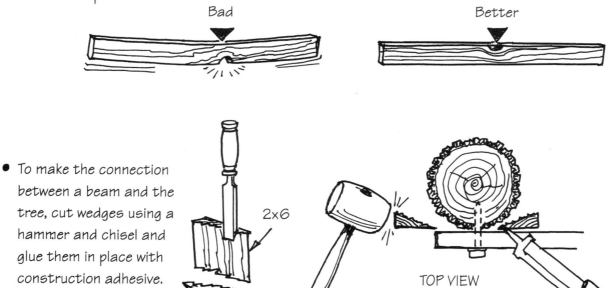

2x6

TOP VIEW

CONSTRUCTION TIPS continued

- Wash your hands immediately if you get any construction adhesive on them. Otherwise, it may not come off for days!

- Predrill an oversize pilot hole in the board you are attaching before mounting it to the tree. Then predrill a slightly smaller hole in the tree if it is a hardwood such as an oak or maple.

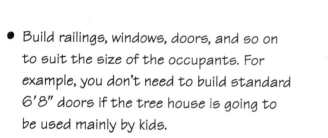

⅜"-dia. pilot hole

washer

½"-dia. lag screw

⅝"-dia. pilot hole

- Build railings, windows, doors, and so on to suit the size of the occupants. For example, you don't need to build standard 6'8" doors if the tree house is going to be used mainly by kids.

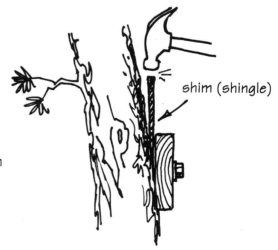

shim (shingle)

- Trees are not always vertical. Therefore, it is sometimes necessary to hammer a wedge or shim between the beam and the tree.

FLOORS & WALLS

FLOORS

Many tree houses suffer from the fact that they are too damp, inviting bugs and rot. Unless you are building a tree house with waterproof walls, windows, and roof, we recommend that you use boards spaced ¼" apart, just as you would if you were building a deck. This will allow any water that gets in the tree house to find its way out quickly. Use lumber sold for decking, such as ⁵⁄₄x6 #2 cedar, and make sure there are supporting joists below, spaced 16" to 24" apart, to nail the decking to.

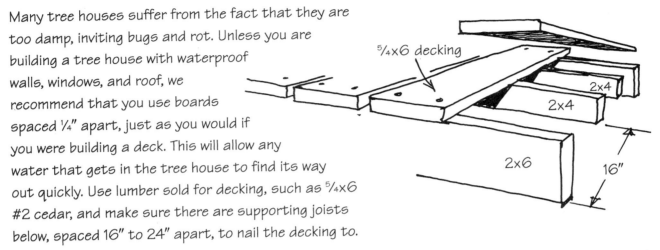

⁵⁄₄x6 decking

2x4

2x4

2x6

16"

WALLS

Walls should be framed with 2x3s or 2x4s to provide support for the siding, windows, and doors.

Walls can be sheathed in either vertical or horizontal siding (boards). Clapboards or shingles are other considerations, but these require plywood subsheathing to be applied first.

Half walls allow lots of air and light to enter the tree house.

vertical siding

horizontal siding

ROOFS

Most wooden roofs should have some sort of finished covering applied to keep out the rain. Ordinary tarpaper is usually sufficient for most tree houses and will last several years. For a more durable solution, use rolled roofing, which is heavier, or asphalt shingles. For a truly elegant (and truly expensive) roof, use wood shingles or shakes.

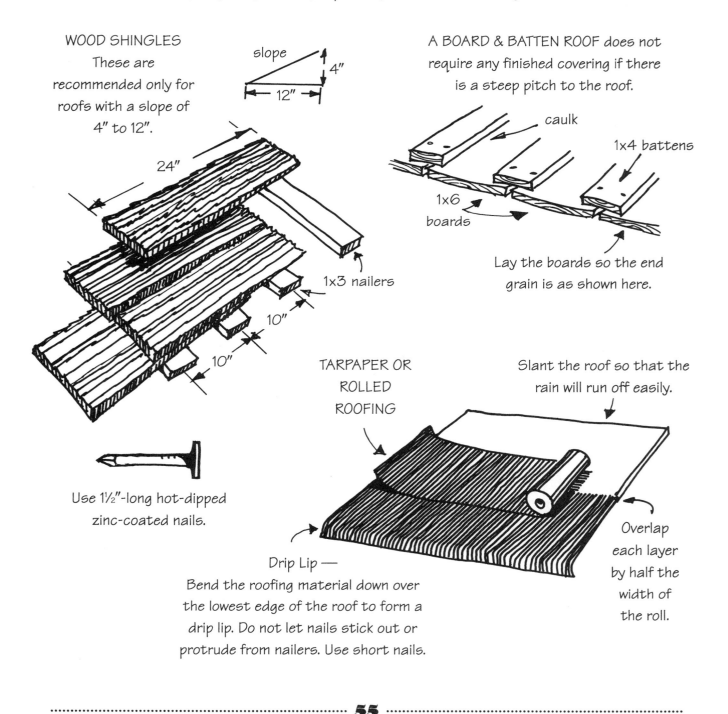

WOOD SHINGLES
These are recommended only for roofs with a slope of 4" to 12".

slope
4"
12"

24"

1x3 nailers

10"

10"

Use 1½"-long hot-dipped zinc-coated nails.

A BOARD & BATTEN ROOF does not require any finished covering if there is a steep pitch to the roof.

caulk

1x4 battens

1x6 boards

Lay the boards so the end grain is as shown here.

TARPAPER OR ROLLED ROOFING

Slant the roof so that the rain will run off easily.

Overlap each layer by half the width of the roll.

Drip Lip —
Bend the roofing material down over the lowest edge of the roof to form a drip lip. Do not let nails stick out or protrude from nailers. Use short nails.

RAILINGS

The height of the railing should be determined by the height of the tree house dweller. Don't make the railing 36" high (adult-size), if the tree house is going to be used mainly by children.

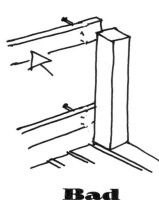 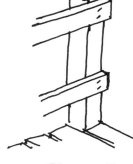 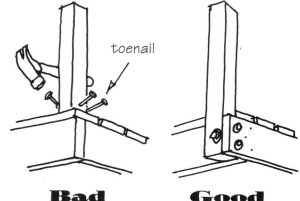

Bad   **Good**   **Bad**   **Good**

If at all possible, keep the rails on the inside of the posts. Otherwise, if the nails become loose, the rails might push out.

Don't toenail the posts to the deck. Instead, run the posts up from the ground or bolt them to the platform frame.

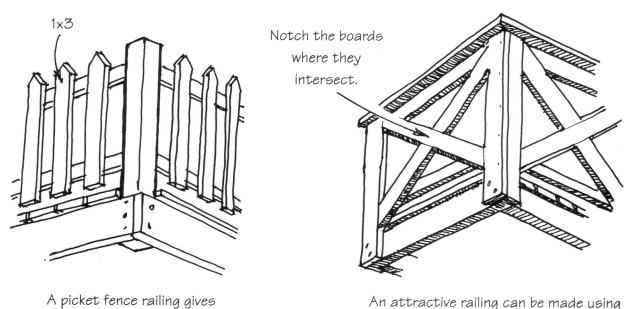

1x3

Notch the boards where they intersect.

A picket fence railing gives both privacy and protection.

An attractive railing can be made using 1x3 spruce glued and screwed together. Triangles add strength to the railing.

DOORS

Doors are useful to keep out squirrels, raccoons, and neighborhood bullies. Here are some suggestions.

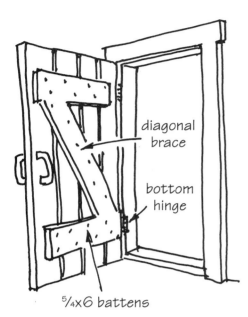

diagonal brace

bottom hinge

⁵⁄₄x6 battens

Make sure the opening is square by taking the diagonal measurements, which should be the same. Make sure the diagonal bracing points toward the bottom hinge.

Tip: To make the job of hanging a door easier, attach the hinges to the door and door trim first. Then place the door in position and nail the door trim to the tree house wall.

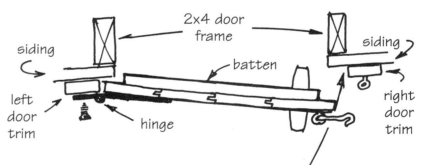

2x4 door frame

siding

batten

siding

left door trim

hinge

right door trim

Make the door ½" wider than the opening on each side. This will provide a stop for the door and also keep out the rain.

DUTCH DOOR

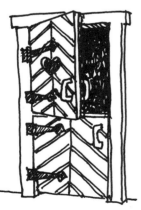

Doors can be fancy, such as this Dutch door made with diagonal tongue-and-groove (T&G) 1x4s glued and nailed to a ½" plywood backboard.

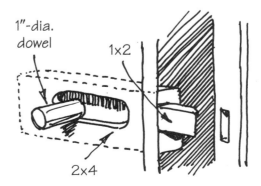

1"-dia. dowel

1x2

2x4

A wooden sliding bolt can be made easily out of scrap lumber.

WINDOWS

Often tree houses suffer from a lack of windows, making the interior dark and clammy. The more windows, the better, but try to avoid using glass, which can be dangerous if broken. Instead, use Plexiglas or just leave the window openings.

Simple shuttered windows can be made out of a few 1x6 T&G boards. Strap hinges are attached on the outside, and the shutters can be hung just like the door (see page 57).

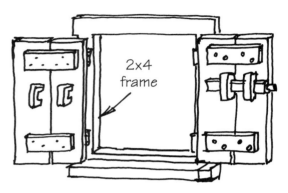

2x4 frame

Wood bar locks the window from inside.

Make your own tilt-in (removable) windows out of 2x2 cedar and ⅛" Plexiglas.
Tilt-in window allows air, but not rain, in.

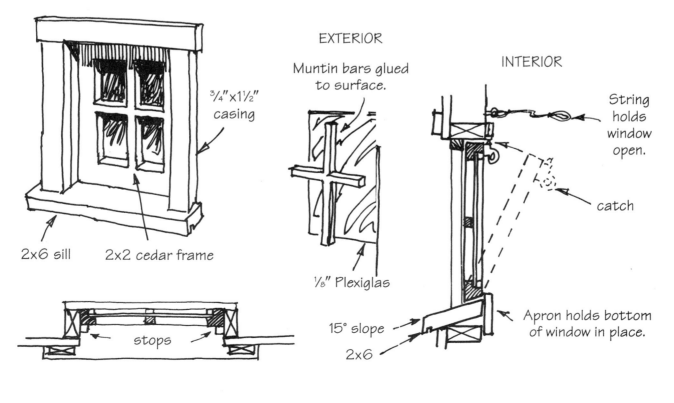

¾"x1½" casing

2x6 sill

2x2 cedar frame

stops

EXTERIOR

Muntin bars glued to surface.

⅛" Plexiglas

15° slope

2x6

INTERIOR

String holds window open.

catch

Apron holds bottom of window in place.

SKYLIGHTS

A skylight allows three times more light into an interior space than a window.
A store-bought one can be quite costly, but you can make your own for just a few dollars.

Choose a pair of rafters between which you want the skylight to go
and cut a rectangular hole. Frame the inside of the hole with 2x6s
so that 2" protrudes above the roof, forming a curb.

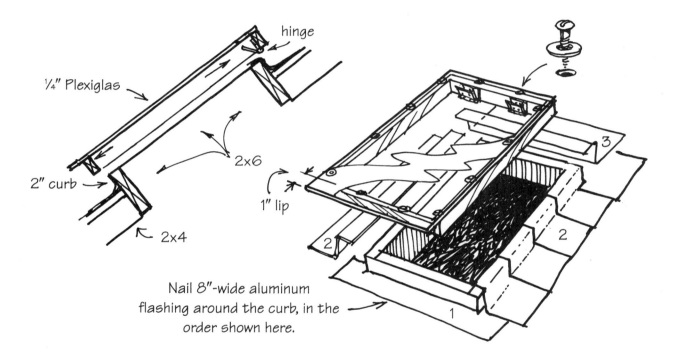

hinge

¼" Plexiglas

2" curb

2x6

1" lip

2x4

3

2

2

1

Nail 8"-wide aluminum
flashing around the curb, in the
order shown here.

Build a frame out of 1x2s to fit loosely around the curb. Cut a piece of ¼" Plexiglas to fit
the frame, allowing a 1" lip at the bottom. Bore ¼" (oversize) holes in the Plexiglas and
screw it to the 1x2 frame, using silicone caulking between the Plexiglas and the frame. If
you want the skylight to provide ventilation or access to the roof, hinge the frame to the
curb at the top, as shown. Otherwise, screw it through the sides to the curb.

If you are using shingles on your roof, place separate pieces
of flashing between the layers of shingles.

Five Basic Designs

That You Can Build

1. A Tree House Built on One Tree

2. A Tree House Built on Two Trees

3. A Tree House Built on Three Trees

4. A Tree House Built on Four Trees (Or Two Trees and Two Posts)

5. The Perch Tree House

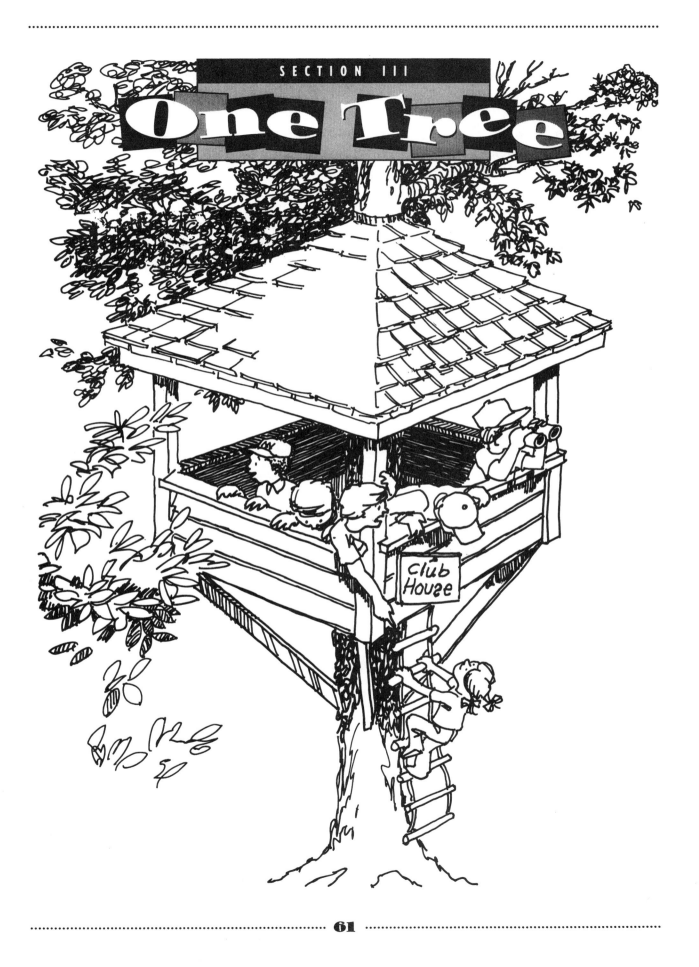

SECTION III

One Tree

Club House

How to Build a Tree House in ONE TREE

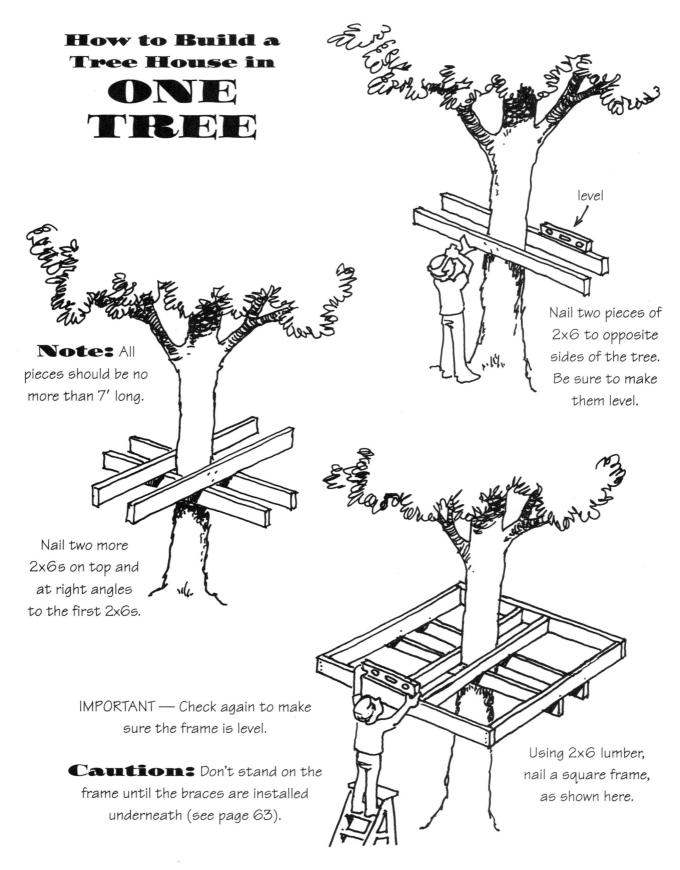

level

Nail two pieces of 2x6 to opposite sides of the tree. Be sure to make them level.

Note: All pieces should be no more than 7' long.

Nail two more 2x6s on top and at right angles to the first 2x6s.

IMPORTANT — Check again to make sure the frame is level.

Caution: Don't stand on the frame until the braces are installed underneath (see page 63).

Using 2x6 lumber, nail a square frame, as shown here.

CORNER BRACES

Cut the four braces (out of 2x4s) to fit the corners, as shown here.

Note: Since the shape of every tree is different, each brace must be cut to length separately.

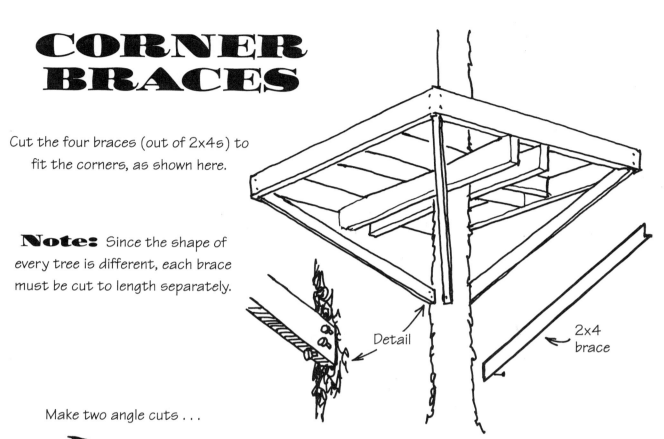

Detail

2x4 brace

Make two angle cuts . . .

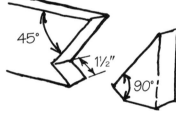

45°

1½"

90°

. . . then cut off the edges at 45° angles so that the braces will fit inside the corners of the frame.

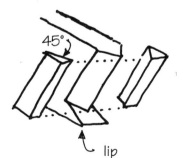

45°

lip

Nail the brace to the inside corner of the frame.

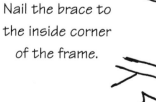

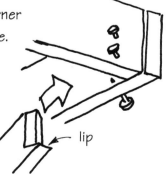

lip

View Looking Down on Corner

brace

THE FLOOR

Fill in between the outer frame with 2x4 bridging so that there is no space larger than 16".

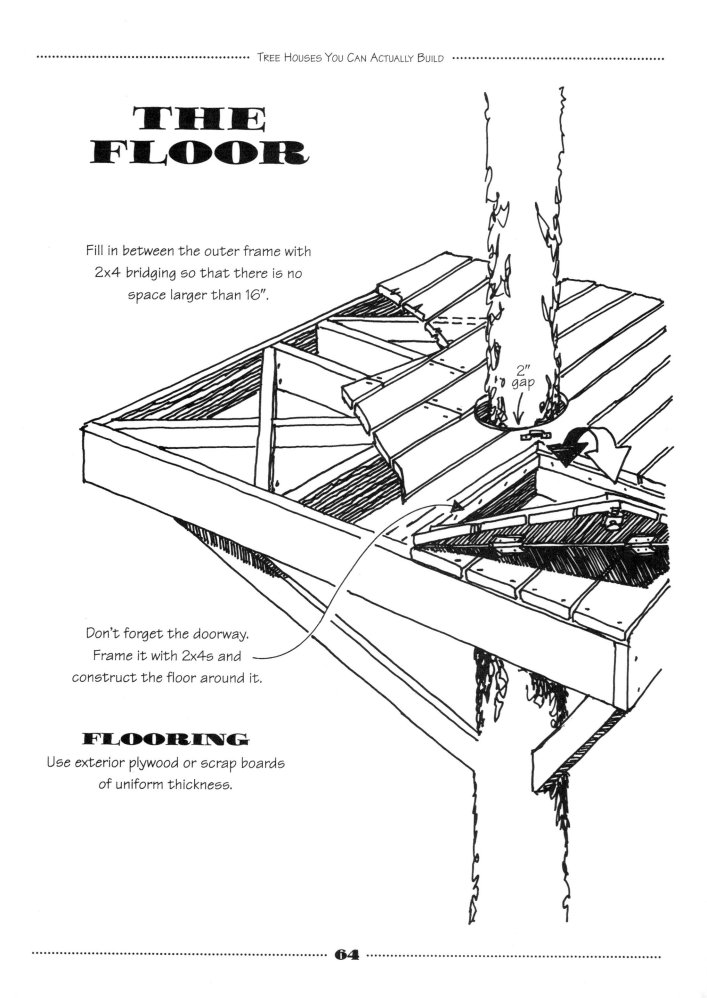

2" gap

Don't forget the doorway. Frame it with 2x4s and construct the floor around it.

FLOORING

Use exterior plywood or scrap boards of uniform thickness.

FRAMING

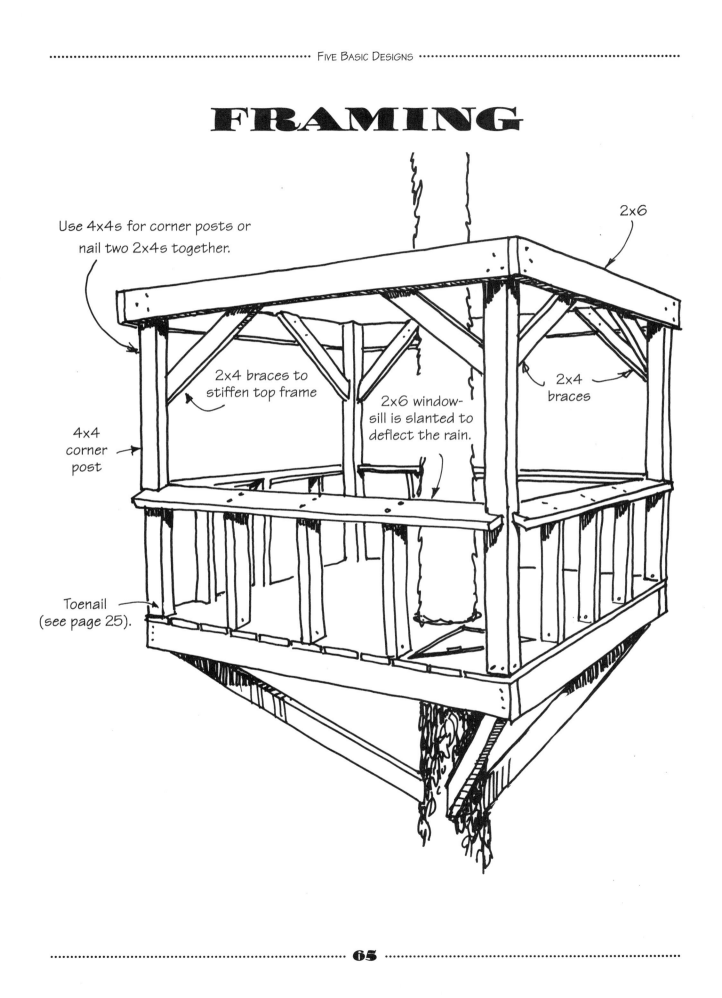

Use 4x4s for corner posts or nail two 2x4s together.

2x6

2x4 braces to stiffen top frame

2x6 window-sill is slanted to deflect the rain.

2x4 braces

4x4 corner post

Toenail (see page 25).

WALLS

You can use plywood or any kind of scrap wood and cover it with shingles. Or you can use plywood or clapboards, as shown here.

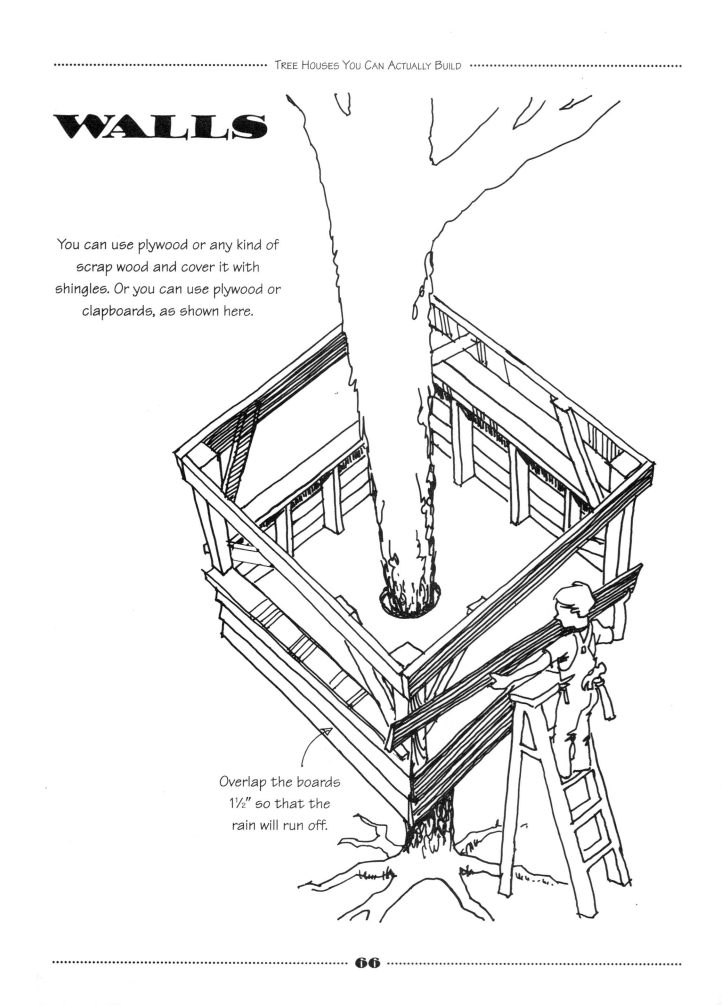

Overlap the boards 1½" so that the rain will run off.

ROOF FRAME

Put up the corner rafters first,
then the rafters in between.

Nail 1x4s across the rafters to provide a
surface for the final roof covering.

See page 55 for roof details.

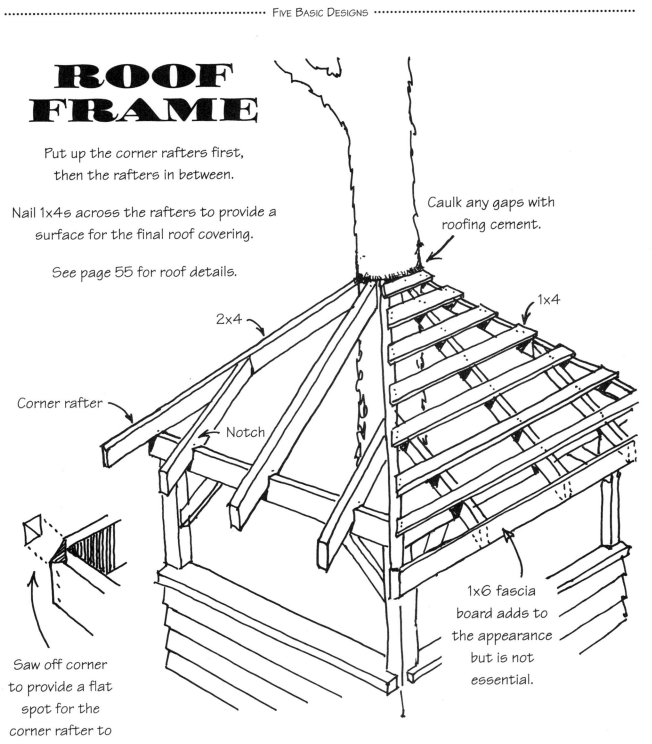

Caulk any gaps with
roofing cement.

2x4

1x4

Corner rafter

Notch

Saw off corner
to provide a flat
spot for the
corner rafter to
rest on.

1x6 fascia
board adds to
the appearance
but is not
essential.

SECTION III

Two Trees

How to Build a Tree House in TWO TREES

SECTION VIEW

Attach two 2x6 beams to two trees with lag screws.

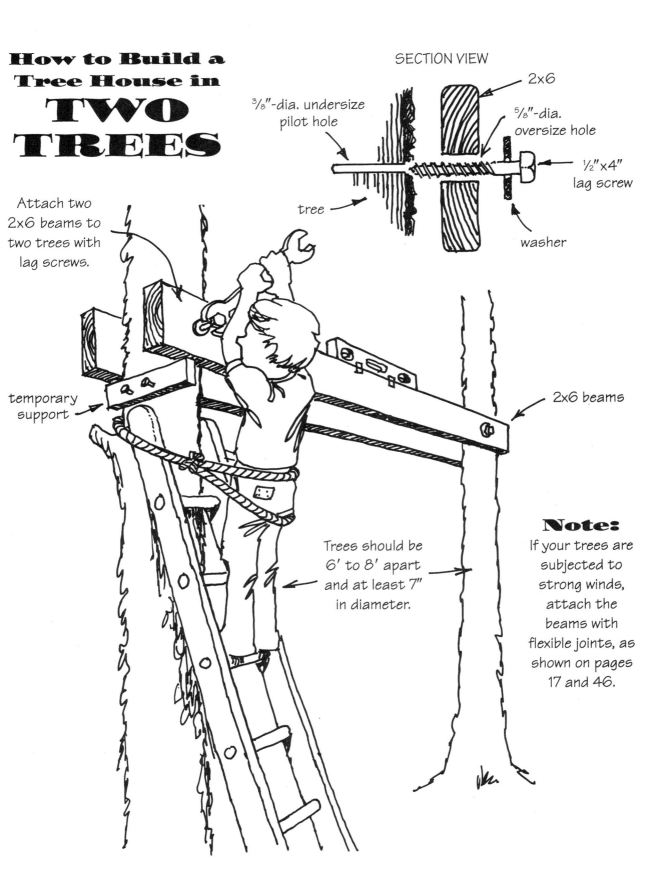

3/8"-dia. undersize pilot hole

tree

2x6

5/8"-dia. oversize hole

1/2"x4" lag screw

washer

temporary support

2x6 beams

Trees should be 6' to 8' apart and at least 7" in diameter.

Note:
If your trees are subjected to strong winds, attach the beams with flexible joints, as shown on pages 17 and 46.

TRIANGLES

Cut six pieces of 2x4 6' long and build two triangular frames.

Cut the tops of the 2x4s so that the triangular frames will overlap each other.

lap joint

Cut halfway through 2x4 and chisel out lap joint.

Bore ½"-dia. holes in all the corners of the triangular frames and bolt the two bottom corners together using ½"x3½" carriage bolts.

2x4 triangular frame

6'

6'

6'

Save leftover piece for one half of the floor.

To make support braces for the beams, use an electric jigsaw to cut out eight triangles from a 4x8 sheet of ¾" exterior plywood. Glue and nail two triangles together to make four pairs.

¾" exterior plywood

jigsaw

6'

8'

2'

2'

1'

3'

Scrap plywood used to make end wall panel.

24"

3½"

12"

5½"

notch

3"

plywood triangular support brace

Cut a 1½"x5½" notch to fit the 2x6 beams.

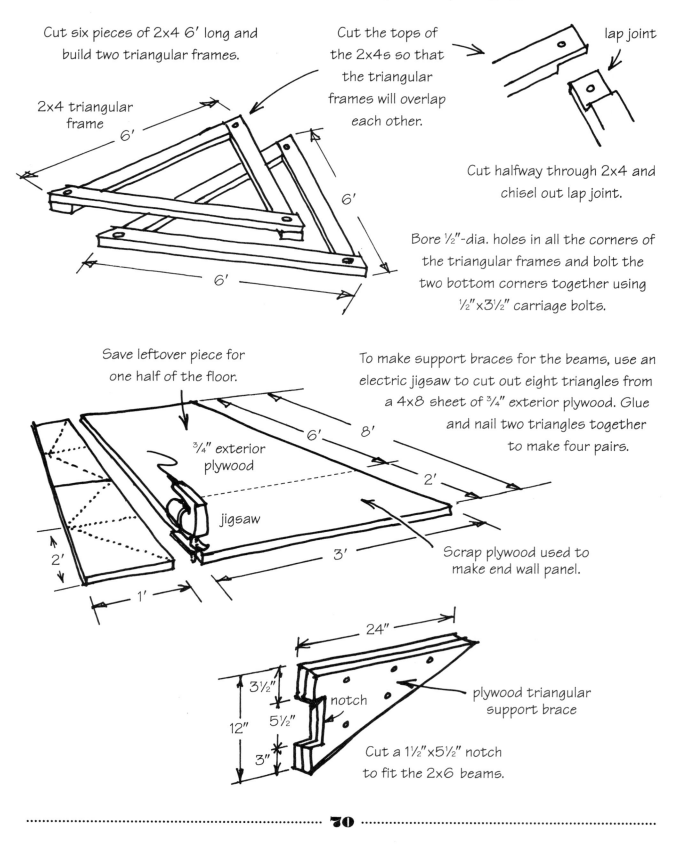

FRAMING
The Tree House

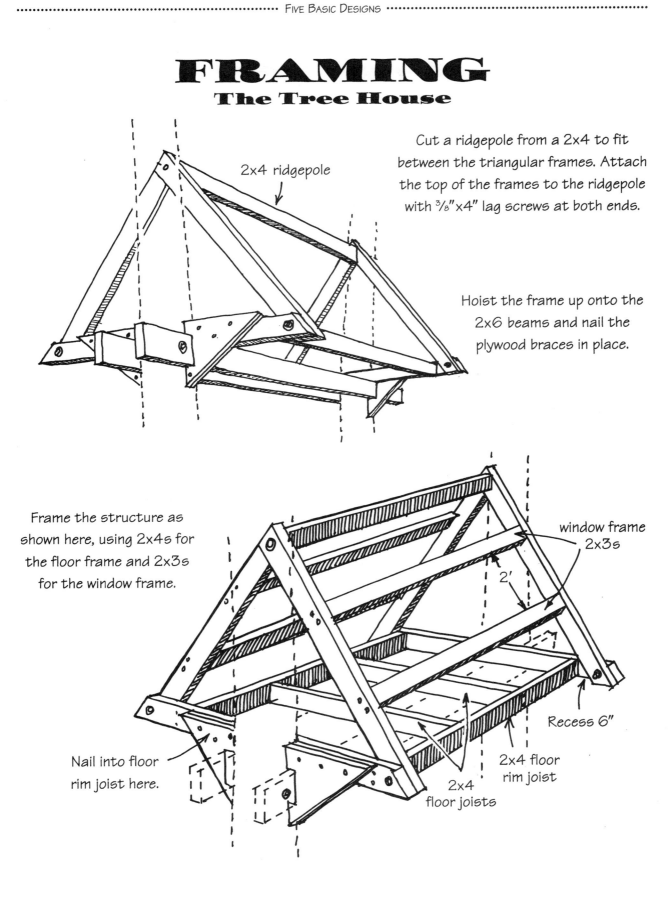

2x4 ridgepole

Cut a ridgepole from a 2x4 to fit between the triangular frames. Attach the top of the frames to the ridgepole with $^3/_8$"x4" lag screws at both ends.

Hoist the frame up onto the 2x6 beams and nail the plywood braces in place.

Frame the structure as shown here, using 2x4s for the floor frame and 2x3s for the window frame.

window frame 2x3s

2'

Recess 6"

Nail into floor rim joist here.

2x4 floor rim joist

2x4 floor joists

FLOOR & WALLS

Floor and end wall panels are cut from two 4x8 sheets of ¾″ exterior plywood.

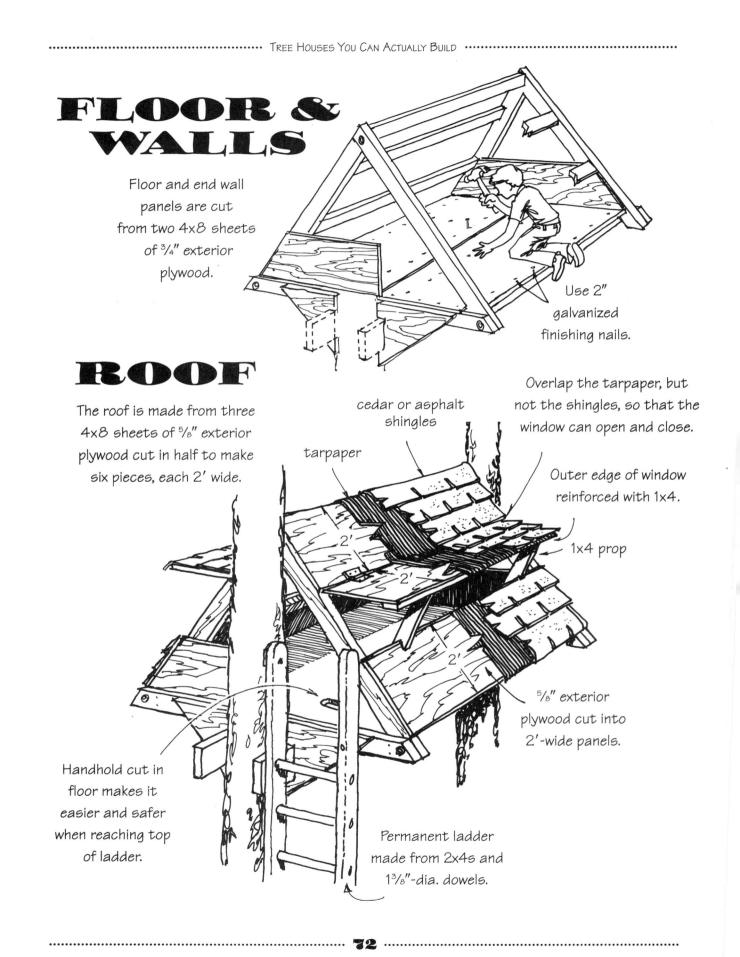

Use 2″ galvanized finishing nails.

ROOF

The roof is made from three 4x8 sheets of ⅝″ exterior plywood cut in half to make six pieces, each 2′ wide.

cedar or asphalt shingles

tarpaper

Overlap the tarpaper, but not the shingles, so that the window can open and close.

Outer edge of window reinforced with 1x4.

1x4 prop

⅝″ exterior plywood cut into 2′-wide panels.

Handhold cut in floor makes it easier and safer when reaching top of ladder.

Permanent ladder made from 2x4s and 1⅜″-dia. dowels.

SECTION III

Three Trees

How to Build a Tree House in
THREE TREES

Quite often you can find three trees growing within 5 to 6 feet of
each other that are well suited for building a tree house. You can use logs
plus sawn lumber, as shown here, or whatever is available.

You will need at least 13 straight logs that are long enough to span the
distance between the trees with 6" additional on each end. Round fence posts
are excellent and can be bought at a nursery, but they tend to be expensive.

Beginning with the largest
log, bore a ½"-dia. hole for
the lag screw 6" down
from the top of each log.

6"

washer

½"-dia. lag screw,
6" to 8" long

Start the lag screw by hammering it through the post and into the tree. Give it several hard whacks, then a quarter turn with a wrench. Continue alternating hammering and turning until the screw is all the way in.

If you are screwing into a hardwood tree, you will need to predrill a pilot hole in the tree slightly smaller than the diameter of the screw.

If you are working up high, you may need to prop the other end up using a forked stick, as shown, or a hoist (see page 26).

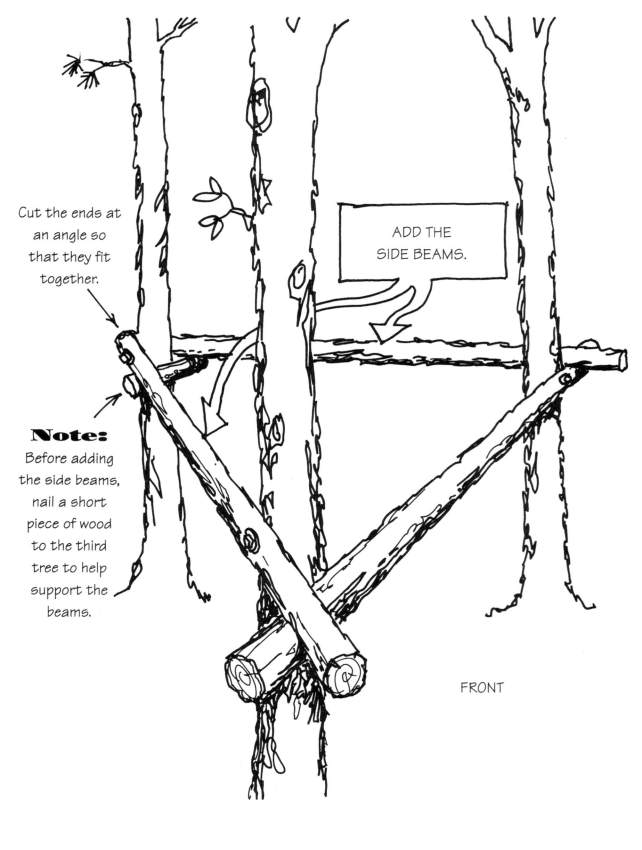

FLOOR

floor boards

Notch the floor
beams if they are
not level.

Add three more floor beams (joists).
Cover the floor beams with boards,
and your platform is finished!

ROOF

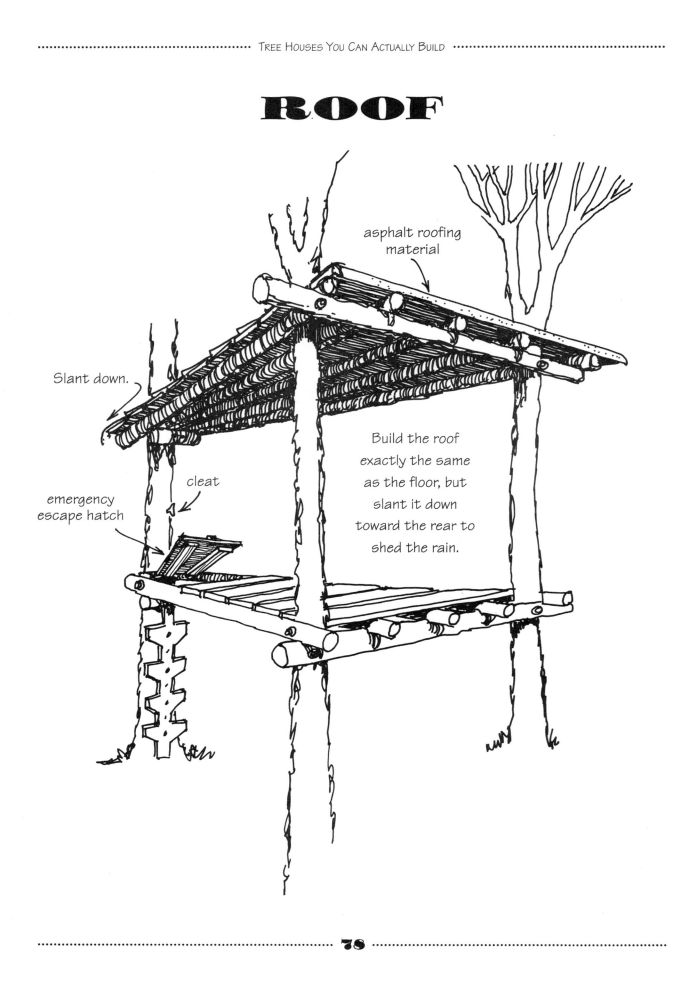

asphalt roofing material

Slant down.

cleat

emergency escape hatch

Build the roof exactly the same as the floor, but slant it down toward the rear to shed the rain.

WALLS

Nail tongue-and-groove (T&G) vertical boards to the floor and roof beams.

ROPE RAILING

Manila rope is okay to use here, since it's not under severe strain.
It also looks better and is cheaper than nylon rope.

Attractive and safe . . .
. . . and you can make this
in 15 minutes.

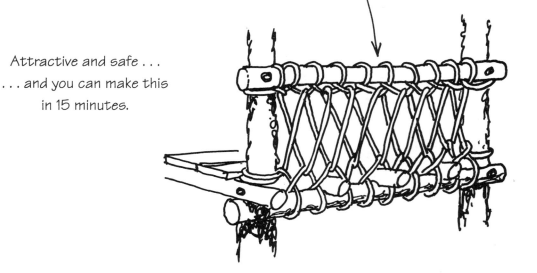

STEP 1.

Make continuous LOOSE loops
4" apart around the top rail.

STEP 2.

On the bottom rail, make loops
identical to the loops on the top rail.

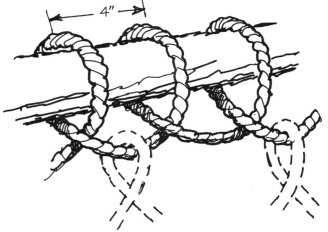

STEP 3.

Weave a third rope through the top
and bottom loops, skipping every other one,
then weave back through the loops
that were skipped.

Four Trees

(OR TWO TREES & TWO POSTS)

THE POSTS

Find two trees approximately 4' to 5' apart.
Measure 6' out from them to form a rectangle or square.

Before installing the posts in the ground, make sure everything is square by measuring the diagonal distances between the posts. (They should be the same.)

For instructions on installing posts, see pages 50–51.

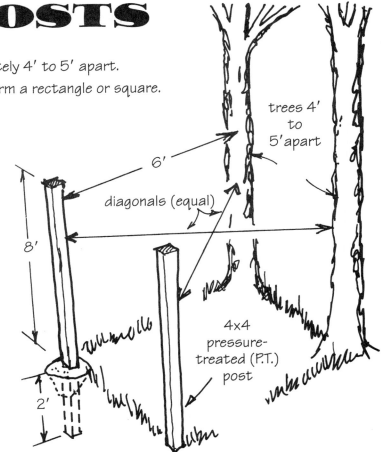

Another way to support a floor frame, especially if the trees are far apart, is to attach the frame to a heavy support beam that has been screwed to the outside of the trees.

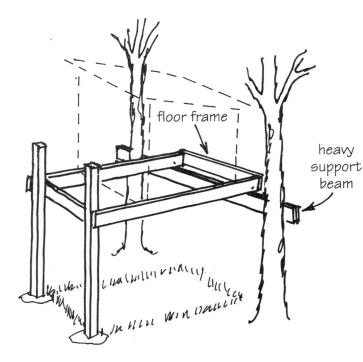

FLOOR FRAME

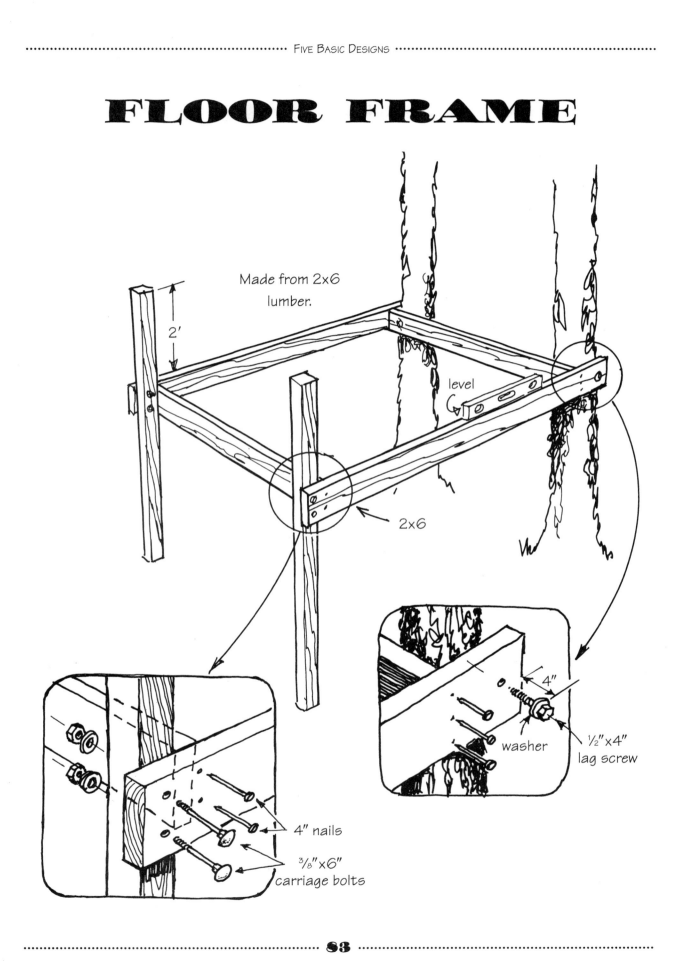

Made from 2x6 lumber.

2'

level

2x6

washer

½"x4" lag screw

4"

4" nails

³⁄₈"x6" carriage bolts

FLOOR PLATFORM

Spaced decking allows any water that enters the tree house to drain out quickly, keeping the interior dry.

2x6 fir floor joists spaced evenly apart.

⁵⁄₄x6 decking spaced ¼" apart.

2' porch

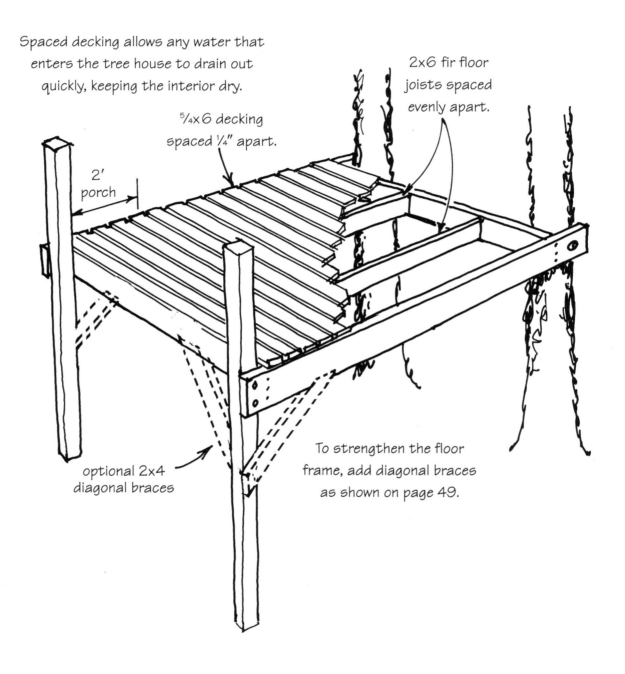

optional 2x4 diagonal braces

To strengthen the floor frame, add diagonal braces as shown on page 49.

WALLS, WINDOWS & ROOF

Framed with 2x4s.

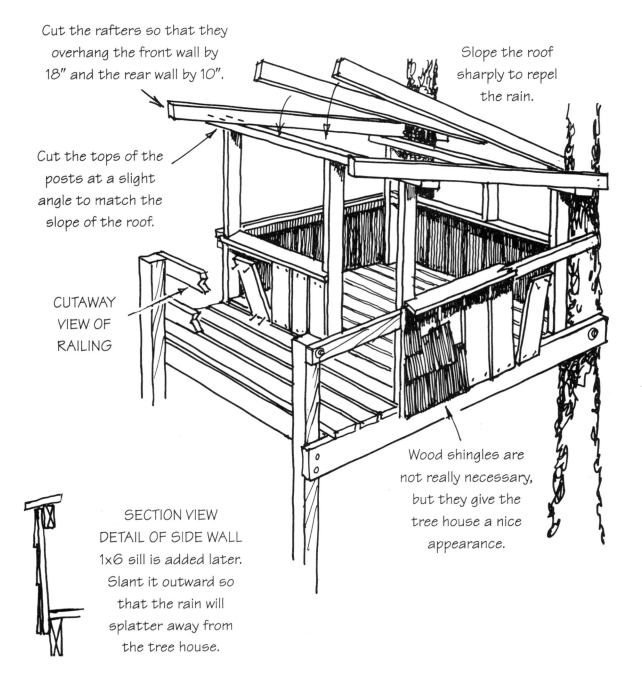

Cut the rafters so that they overhang the front wall by 18" and the rear wall by 10".

Cut the tops of the posts at a slight angle to match the slope of the roof.

Slope the roof sharply to repel the rain.

CUTAWAY VIEW OF RAILING

SECTION VIEW DETAIL OF SIDE WALL 1x6 sill is added later. Slant it outward so that the rain will splatter away from the tree house.

Wood shingles are not really necessary, but they give the tree house a nice appearance.

ROOF

THATCH the roof with bundles of straw tied onto 1x2 crosspieces.
Begin at the bottom and work up, overlapping the previous layer as much as possible.

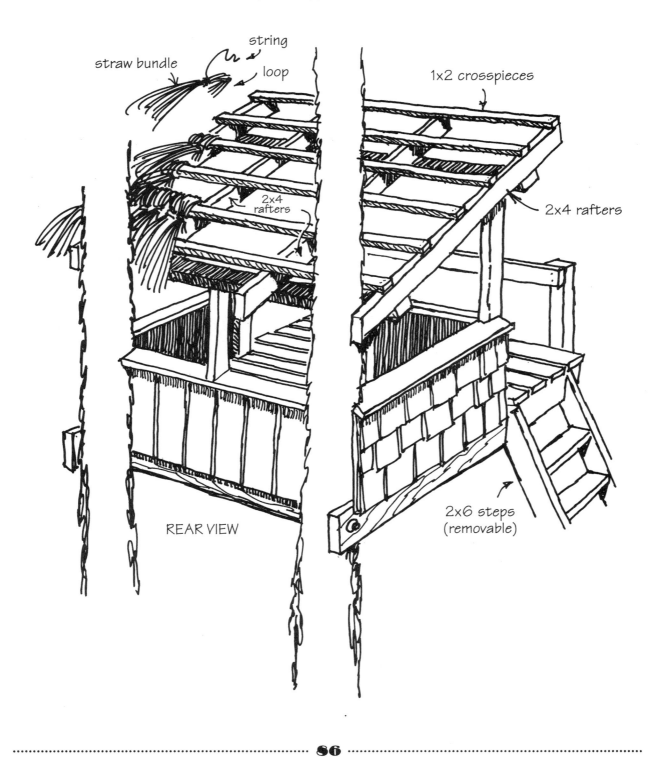

string

straw bundle

loop

1x2 crosspieces

2x4 rafters

2x4 rafters

REAR VIEW

2x6 steps
(removable)

The Perch

TREE HOUSE

Triangles are the key to building a strong structure. This tree house, which is built on one tree, uses triangles wherever possible.

The platform can be built in a day. The circular stairs provide easy access for both adults and small children.

To Frame the
PERCH TREE HOUSE

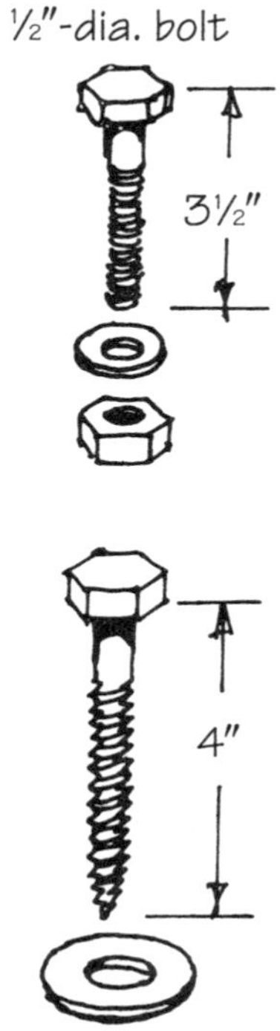

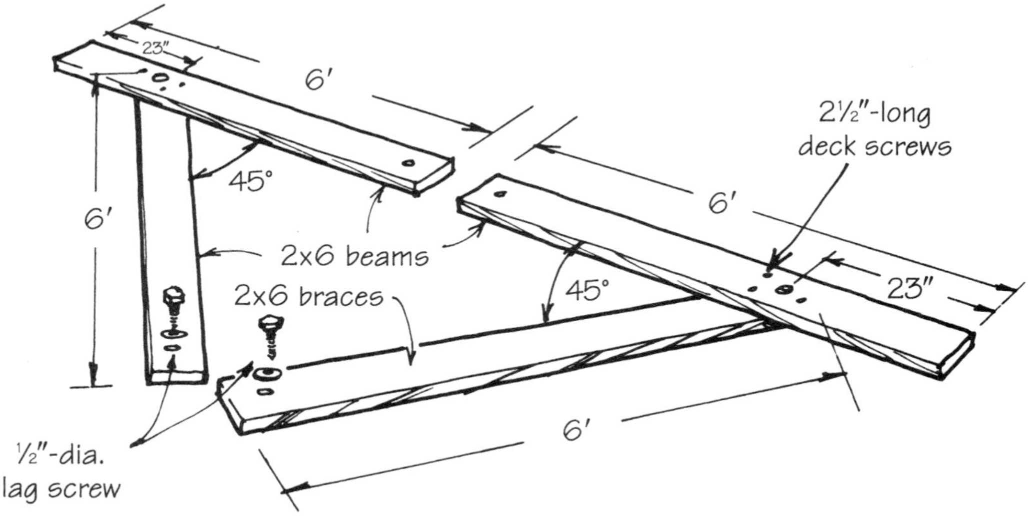

½"-dia. bolt

3½"

½"-dia. lag screw

4"

23"

6'

6'

45°

2x6 beams

2x6 braces

½"-dia. lag screw

45°

6'

6'

23"

2½"-long deck screws

Build two sets of braces and beams on the ground. Bolt the ends of the braces to the beams using ½"x3½" bolts. Add three 2½"-long deck screws to keep the pieces from pivoting.

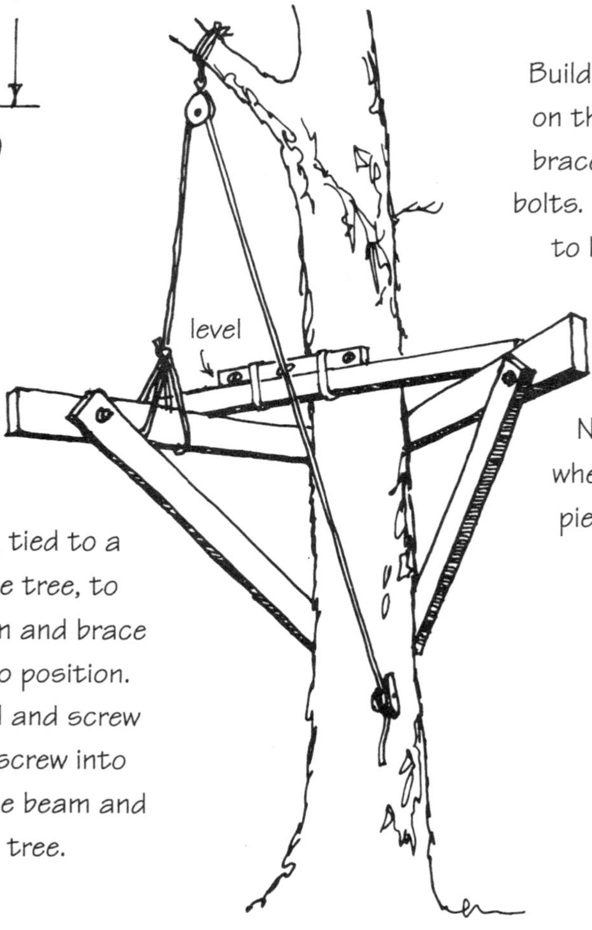

level

Use a pulley, tied to a branch in the tree, to hoist the beam and brace assembly into position. Check for level and screw a ½"x4" lag screw into each end of the beam and into the tree.

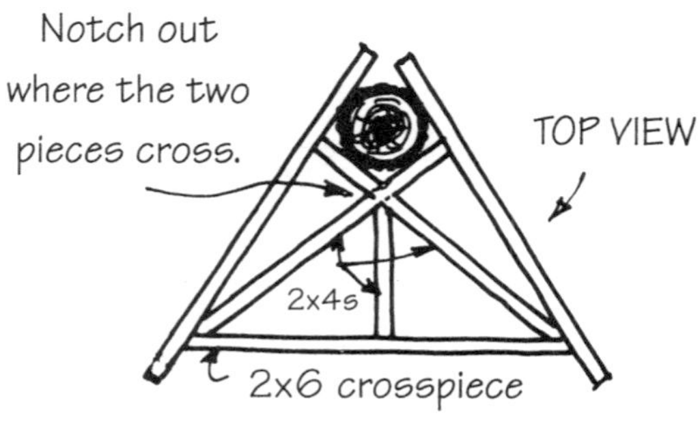

Notch out where the two pieces cross.

TOP VIEW

2x4s

2x6 crosspiece

Add a 2x6 crosspiece. Frame in the center with 2x4s to provide support for the floorboards.

FLOORING

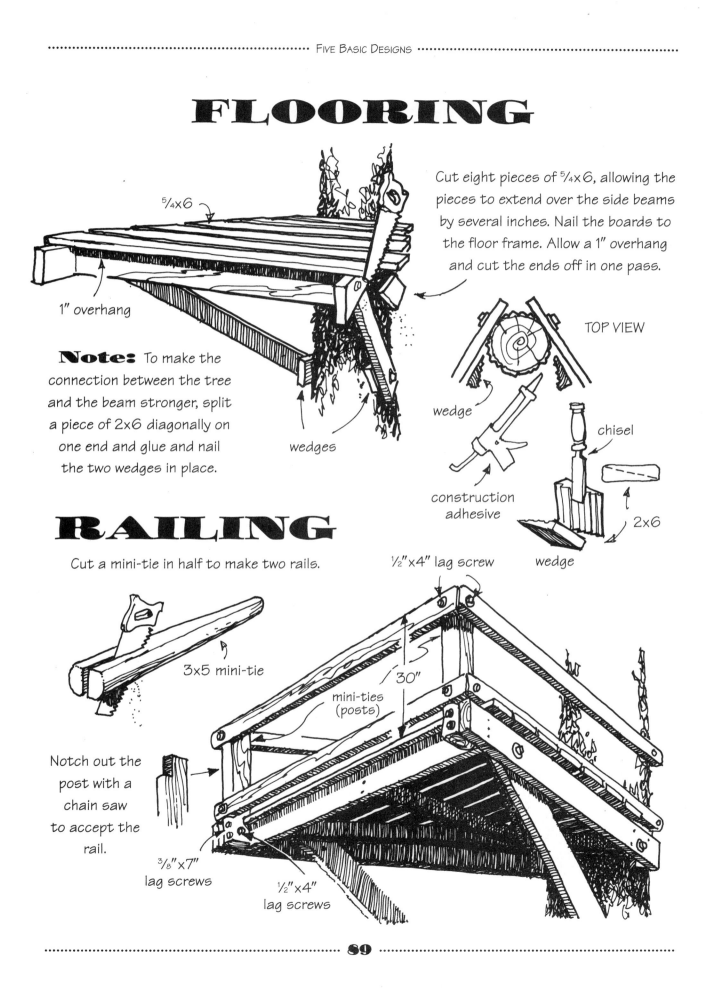

Cut eight pieces of ⁵⁄₄x6, allowing the pieces to extend over the side beams by several inches. Nail the boards to the floor frame. Allow a 1" overhang and cut the ends off in one pass.

⁵⁄₄x6

1" overhang

Note: To make the connection between the tree and the beam stronger, split a piece of 2x6 diagonally on one end and glue and nail the two wedges in place.

wedges

TOP VIEW

wedge

construction adhesive

chisel

2x6

wedge

½"x4" lag screw

RAILING

Cut a mini-tie in half to make two rails.

3x5 mini-tie

Notch out the post with a chain saw to accept the rail.

mini-ties (posts)

30"

³⁄₈"x7" lag screws

½"x4" lag screws

ROPE

gives the appearance of a Robinson Crusoe tree house
and at the same time provides security for small children.

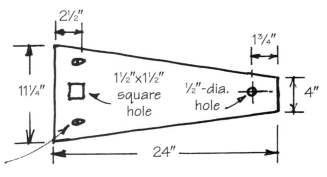

Bore a ¾"-dia. hole
2" deep and insert
one end of a rope.
Hold it in place
with a screw.

The rope goes
inside to
outside, crosses
itself, then goes
to the next rail.

CIRCULAR STAIRS

wrap around the tree and are fairly easy to make.
(Recommended for large trees only — minimum 20"-dia. trunk.)

Measure the distance from the ground to
the top of the deck and divide by 9" to
find out how many steps you will need.
Each step is a 2x12 cut 24" long. Multiply
the number of steps by 2' to find out how
much 2x12 lumber you will need.

½"-dia. angled holes
(see next page).

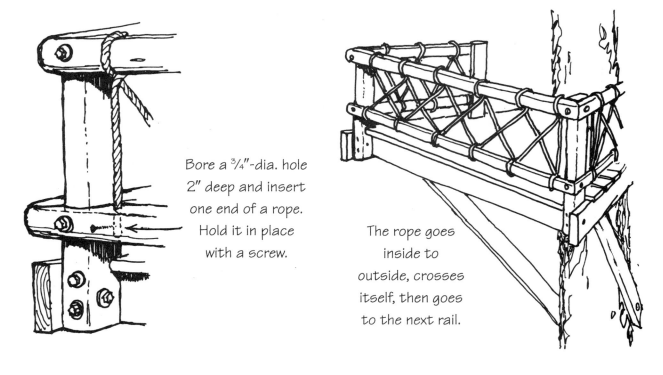

2½"

1¾"

11¼"

1½"x1½"
square
hole

½"-dia.
hole

4"

24"

STEPS

Each step is held to the tree by a ½"-dia. bolt attached to a ⅜"x4" screw eye drilled into the tree. The step is supported from the bottom by two 34"-long pieces of ½" reinforcing bar (rebar).

½"x2½"
galvanized bolt

2x12 step

45°

⅜"x4"
screw eye

½" rebar

34"

45°

1"

level

½" rebar

Cut out a 1½"x1½" square hole 1" from the end of each step to hold the baluster.

Drill two ½"-dia. holes at a 45° angle in the underside of each step, 2½" from the end of the step. Use a 45° triangle as a guide.

2½"

45°

1"

INSTALLING THE STEPS

Starting at the top of the platform, measure down 9" to find the position for the top of the last step. Measure down another 2" to allow for the thickness of materials and drill a ¼"-dia. pilot hole 3" deep for the screw eye. Using a short piece of rebar for leverage, screw a ⅜"x4½" screw eye into the tree.

Mount the step onto the screw eye using a ½"x2½" galvanized bolt, washer, and nut.

Slip the two pieces of rebar into the angled holes in the underside of the steps and mark where the bottom ends of the rebar touch the tree. Drill a ½"-dia. hole 1" above the marks and approximately 1½" deep into the tree. Place the bottom ends of the rebar into the tree holes and check to see if the step is level. Adjust, if necessary, by drilling deeper holes. (Fill the holes in the steps with construction adhesive and place the top ends of the rebar into the holes.)

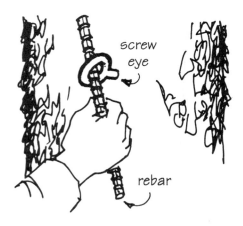

screw eye

rebar

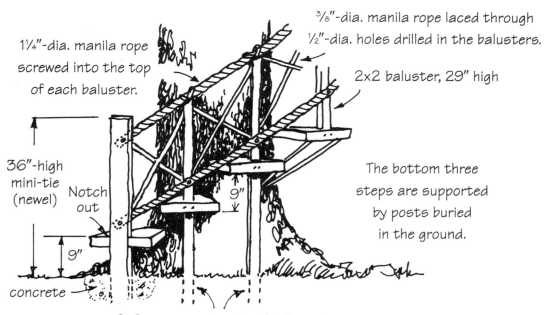

⅜"-dia. manila rope laced through ½"-dia. holes drilled in the balusters.

1¼"-dia. manila rope screwed into the top of each baluster.

2x2 baluster, 29" high

36"-high mini-tie (newel)

Notch out

9"

The bottom three steps are supported by posts buried in the ground.

9"

concrete

2x2 pressure-treated (P.T.) post

SECTION · IV

More Ideas

EXTRA TIPS

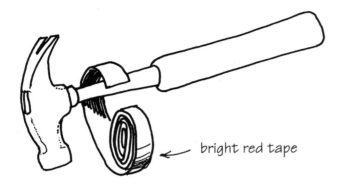

← bright red tape

Tools can get lost very easily in the woods, so clear the area where you will be working of leaves and twigs before you begin. As an added precaution, spray the handles of your tools white or wrap a piece of bright red tape around them.

It is very handy to have something to hold on to when you are climbing into a tree house. A handhold cut in the floor can serve this purpose.

handhold

Spray for moths and insects early in the summer so that they won't build nests in the tree house.

PLEASE HELP KEEP OUR TREE HOUSE CLEAN THANK YOU

WASTE

Tree houses have a way of getting dirty very fast. Keep a small whiskbroom hanging from a nail and build a trash door for sweeping out sticks, leaves, and dirt.

ROPE BRIDGE

If you are lucky enough to have more than one tree house, here is how you can bridge the gap.

Note: A total of four separate ropes span the distance between the tree houses so that if one breaks, the other three will take the load.

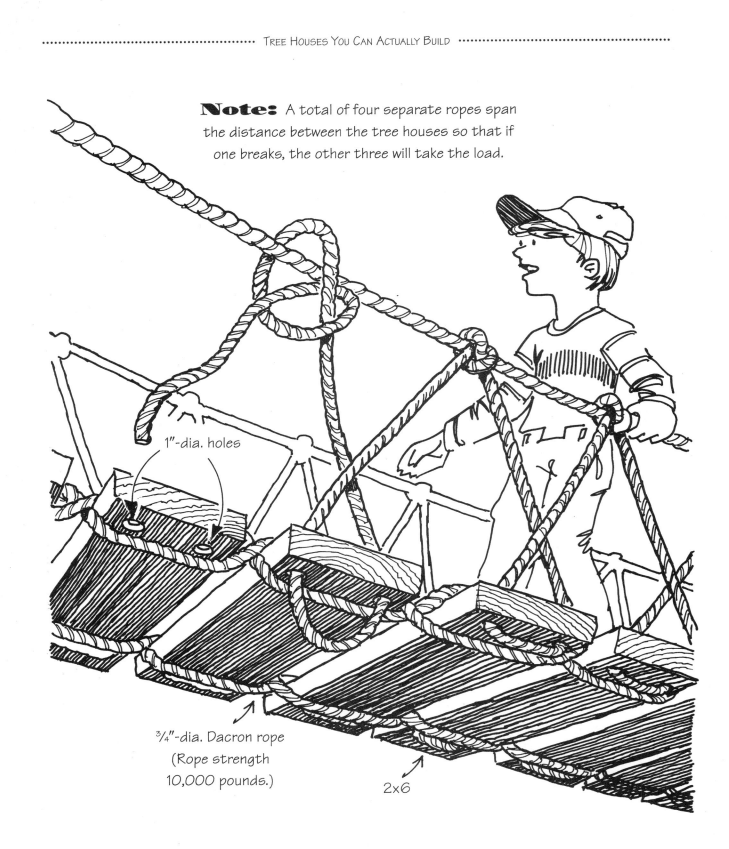

1"-dia. holes

³/₄"-dia. Dacron rope
(Rope strength
10,000 pounds.)

2x6

Stiles' Shingled Tree House *(right)*

Our tree house has weathered three kids and all their neighborhood friends. It has grown, changed, and been repaired many times and now sports a new lookout perch to view the harbor. This tree house, supported by two oaks, has lots of extras, including an emergency escape hatch, a mail drop, and a pulley with a basket for bringing up lunch and supplies. The ivy-covered lattice sides camouflage our pool pump. Look closely for the crocodile and dolphin that David carved at the ends of the roof trim.

Tree House on Stilts with Blue Tarp Roof *(below left)*

This action-packed tree house is usually filled with kids and was designed for several activities. The pitched roof is covered with a blue tarp, which allows light to filter through, and swings hang from the floor and to the side of the house. A basketball hoop is attached to the outside of the slatted railing, and a trolley extends from two nearby trees. The house was built from wood salvaged from the beach in East Hampton, Long Island. The support posts are buried in cement in the ground, and there is plenty of room underneath the tree house to store bikes and other play equipment.

Pirate Ship Tree House
(below right)

If you like intricate angles and boat building, try this 24-foot-long tree house, which is bolted together and uses not one straight piece of lumber. The builder made plans and blueprints and, with the help of his son, lifted the heavy, 24-foot pressure-treated beams into position. A rope bridge connects the ship to the second floor of a shed, where the kids can sleep. A figurehead of a dragon is carved on the "bow" of the tree house, which more often than not is manned by at least four mates.

Tree House in the Mountains *(left)*

The owner of this tree house built it on a hill in New York State and deeded it to his four grandchildren. "No adults are allowed without permission; however, the owners are generous." The tree house is supported by five tree trunks and is accessed by a sturdy staircase. It is Gothic in detail, with an "eyebrow" door. The windows were obtained from the lumberyard, which gave the builder a special deal on an odd lot. The exterior wood is stained green, and the shingled roof has weathered to blend in with the woods.

Simple Platform Tree House *(below left)*

This platform tree house is built high up in a giant, sprawling beech tree with a trunk almost 5 feet in diameter and gnarled, aboveground roots. Two railings enclose the platform, which is reached by a removable homemade ladder, constructed from 2x4s. A monkey rope stretches from this tree house to another one at a different level in a nearby tree, creating a lofty village. The architect of this tree house used restraint in design so as not to compromise the ancient qualities of this majestic tree, so perfect for climbing.

Pine Log Tree Fort *(below right)*

After clearing out trees in a pine forest to make a play area for his son, Zachary, Gene found that the town would take only the brush away, leaving the logs on his property. This inspired him to build a tree fort out of the pine logs. With the bark left on the logs, this rustic tree house is nicely camouflaged, perched at the edge of the woods. The entire fort is made from cedar logs, which range in diameter from 1 to 6 inches.

Sunburst Tree House (right)

The Siegel family designed their tree house to nestle inside the five "arms" of a black mulberry tree on their property. After several early-morning meetings at the breakfast table and much brainstorming, they made a list of criteria for the perfect tree house: • Respect the tree and not harm it in any way. • Stairs for Dakota, the dog, and the three boys (ages 5, 7, and 9). • Little decks for hiding out. • A secret entrance. • Dutch doors for spying. • A skylight for sleeping under the stars. • Bunk beds. • Enough windows to keep watch but not sacrifice privacy. • A sunburst theme repeated on the peak and railing. • A tire swing. The tree house was a labor of love, a combination of the entire family's input.

Multilevel Tree House (below left)

This beautifully crafted tree house, built out of mahogany and secured with stainless steel nails, was designed by an architect and built by a contractor and carpenter. A statuesque beech tree stands in the center of the tree platform, its outstretched arms emerging through the floor at either side. The lumber was carved out to accept the shape of the tree, allowing extra room for growth. Clear 4x4 cedar posts support the platform, extending through the floor and becoming railing supports. A slide, swings, and a cargo net are all part of the tree house. For safety and a soft landing, a mulch of wood chips covers the ground.

The Playhouse (below right)

Because the mother of these kids works at home, she installed an intercom inside the tree house so she can talk to her kids from her home office. This sturdy tree house is built of stained, pressure-treated wood. It features Dutch doors, a working window with shutters, and an emergency escape hatch, leading to a sandbox underneath. The tree house is on stilts, with a tree growing through the center of the top deck. Both decks are surrounded by protective railings. The bottom deck is a favorite place for the family dog to hang out.

Dr. Seuss Tree House (left)

If Dr. Seuss were to design and build a tree house, it might look like this — with a crooked stovepipe chimney and a shed roof shingled with cedar shakes. The square-framed house sits atop a triangular base and is supported by a sturdy sycamore tree and two posts. A triangular deck with a slatted railing (just tall enough to be safe) projects off to one side. The wood siding is stained leaf green. The design and building of this whimsical tree house was a joint effort of a group of friends who built it for Benjamin's birthday. They discovered that lumberyard and hardware salesmen were extremely helpful and eager to answer their questions once they found out a tree house was being built. Now Benjamin and Alexander spend hours aloft. The house's safety features include strong stainless steel handles at the top of the ladder, a protective railing, and a soft ground cover of tree bark mulch.

Lief Anne and Vanessa
(below left)

Tea for two in a tree house.

Granddad's Four-Level Platform Tree House
(below right)

Robby's grandfather began building this tree house for his grandson as the family was moving into their main house. It is composed of a series of four platforms at different levels, built around four oak trees. The top platform is triangular, with two railings around the perimeter. Since Robby is only three years old, the tree house was designed with the top platform only 8 feet above the ground. The structure evolved, like most tree houses, over a period of time. Robby's grandfather began with the top level, added to it, and then attached a slide to the midlevel platform. The leaves of the trees form a canopy around the structure in the summer.

Tree House with Skylight *(above)*

This tree house took a summer to build and was constructed entirely from wood that was salvaged from the discarded boardwalk of Robert Moses State Park on Long Island. The builders, two brothers and their nephew, used no plans, beginning with only a platform and letting the more complex house evolve gradually as they found more materials. The tree grows right through the roof of the house. So far, no rainwater has leaked through the tarpaper wrapped around the branches. A Plexiglas skylight, attached at the top with one nail, pivots open to catch a breeze. The interior is filled with two bunk beds, a table, a refrigerator, and a TV. A gangplank ladder leads to a trap door in the floor of the house.

Virginia's Tree Perch *(right)*

This tree perch was built by the authors for Virginia, who requested that the access be by circular stairs that wrap around the tree trunk. The steps were made out of 2x12 treads, supported by ½-inch-diameter reinforcement bar (rebar). The intricate rope work not only serves as a handhold but also gives the tree house a Robinson Crusoe look. With no roof, there is a great view of the sky and a feeling that you are part of the tree. To accommodate the steps, we chose a sturdy, upright tree with a thick trunk free of lower branches. The platform is framed with 2x6s, which support ⅝x6 decking. This is a terrific tree house for a person of any age — a perch for bird watching, stargazing, or daydreaming.

Tree House in Progress *(left)*

This simple structure is proof positive that a tree house does not have to be a costly, involved construction project. This beautiful maple tree begged for a tree house, and Harrison Waterstreet used leftover scraps of wood to construct it in just a few hours. Although the freeform design is still evolving, the tree house is sufficient as is to be a refuge for an artist or a playhouse for friends.

Tree House on the Beach
(below left)

Built on stilts, surrounded by trees, and with a view of the Atlantic Ocean, this tree house is perfect for kids and adults. It's ideal for meditating, writing, or simply watching the sun set. The wood has weathered to a soft gray, and the place is filled with the scent of wild honeysuckle. This is a tree house that one could imagine living in forever.

Tree House on an Old Logging Trail *(below right)*

A carpenter was hired to build the platform and supports for this tree house. The remaining work was done by two brothers, a sister, and their neighborhood friends, who have made it an ongoing project for the past five years. When inspired, they get together to add a new wall, shingles, or a salvaged window. Most of the wood was scrap, found at a local lumberyard. The tree house is supported by three trees and sits in the middle of what used to be a logging road, lined with majestic pine trees on either side. The sun filters through the pine needles, casting a soft, subtle glow on the house at dusk.

Villa Gorilla Tree House *(above)*

The owners of this tree house started out with the idea of raising an old fishing boat up into a tree. Instead, they ended up having a friend, Jeff Adee, a master woodworker, build this carefully crafted log tree house from wood left over from a previous building project. The honey-colored, custom-milled logs are joined using Swedish coped joints. The interior has a cathedral ceiling and a sleeping loft, which is accessed by a log ladder made by notching out flat steps from a single log. The roof is covered with hand-split cedar shakes. The tree house stands on braced logs embedded in the ground and has a gigantic oak tree growing through the deck, shading the house.

Whirligig Tree House *(right)*

This tree house is enveloped by a tree and decorated with whirligigs. The ladder creates different levels to perch on, inviting children to continue climbing until they reach the house. The design is an open, airy one, with space between the floorboards to prevent water from pooling and rotting the wood. All the joints are glued and screwed together, creating a very strong structure. As in many tree houses, the stairs were the last thing to be built.

Tree House with Five Tree Trunks and Platform/Deck *(left)*

This fanciful tree house took the Glassman family four days to build, with the help of a carpenter friend. They started by erecting a platform 7 feet up from the ground in a majestic sycamore tree. Out of respect for the tree, they left it completely intact. Since they expected much of the activity to take place outside on the deck, they designed a large wraparound platform. After securing the deck with braces and attaching a rope railing around the perimeter, they built a tree house in the middle of the platform, incorporating the five tree trunks into the design. The trunks emerge through holes cut in the sides of the house that are large enough to allow extra room as the tree grows in diameter. Sun filters through the circular cut-out windows and the skylight, which hinges open. The peaked roof is covered with slatted wood, and the ceiling is high enough for an adult to stand inside. A rope ladder leads to a trap door in the deck. The Glassmans designed two other secret entrances, one through a sliding door in the back and another in the floor of the tree house. It can be reached by climbing up sturdy log steps, which are lodged and toenailed against the braces and the tree trunks at the exact spots where the children's footsteps reached. Log benches and a log table support a lamp. When the wind blows, the tree house sways, rocking the kids to sleep in their bunk beds.

MICHAEL TRUSTY

Katie's Santa Fe Hacienda *(left)*

Does a tree house have to be in a tree? In New Mexico, where trees are scarce, a stockade fence serves the same purpose, supporting the Trusty family's "tree" house, which stands 7 feet off the ground. With a 360-degree view of the Sandia Mountains, this airy tree house is open above the slatted railing and has a cedar-shingled roof to shade desert dwellers from the sun. The sides were constructed from 1x6 cedar fencing cut up and fit in between 4x4 posts, and the roof was framed using 2x4 construction wood. It was designed by Katie, who wanted a playhouse with "stirs" [stairs]. A sturdy "stir" ladder is attached to the front entranceway. The family planted vines to grow up the sides, creating their own ivy-covered refuge, and decorated the railings with tiny Christmas lights. They have spent many nights in the tree house, which fits two sleeping bags comfortably.

CROW'S NEST

2x6

¾" exterior plywood

Find a strong branch on a tree that is at least 10" thick where it joins the trunk. Choose a place that is level — where two branches fork out from the main branch — and nail a half barrel to the branches. Using 2x6 lumber and ¾" exterior plywood, build steps leading up to the barrel, as shown here.

FIRE POLE

A quick way to exit a tree house is to slide down a fire pole. Make one out of a piece of 3"-dia. plastic pipe attached to the top of the tree house and cemented into the ground below.

EMERGENCY ESCAPE HATCH

Every tree house needs an emergency escape hatch to provide a quick exit in case neighborhood bullies or an animal gains access.

3"-dia. plastic pipe

concrete

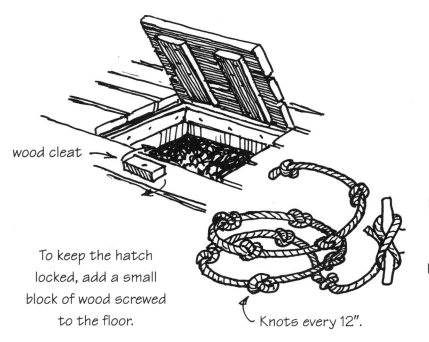

wood cleat

To keep the hatch locked, add a small block of wood screwed to the floor.

Knots every 12".

Provide a ¾"-dia. nylon rope inside the tree house for emergency escapes. Disguise the escape hatch so that no one knows about it except you.

TREE HOUSE FURNITURE

Bench

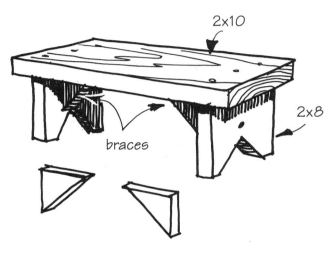

2x10

braces

2x8

Table

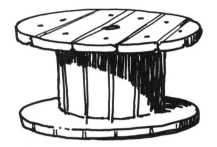

A spool used by utility companies to wrap cable can often be found at the dump.

Table

scrap plywood

fruit box

Chair with Storage

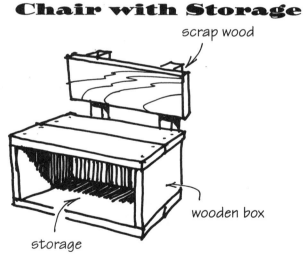

scrap wood

storage

wooden box

Chair

Tree stump cut with a chain saw.

Scrap Wood Chair

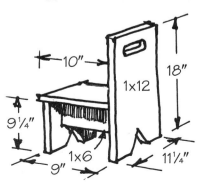

10"

18"

1x12

9¼"

1x6

9"

11¼"

BEDS

For large tree houses, rope beds can be made using 4x4s for the legs and 2x6s for the frame.

2x6

4x4

¼"-dia. rope spaced every 3".

mattress

For smaller tree houses, a 2"-thick foam rubber mattress will do fine.

Hammocks are comfortable and take up very little space.

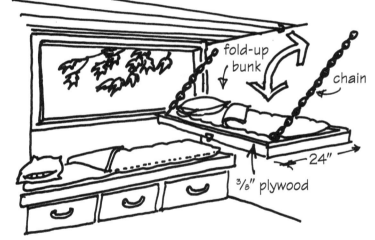

fold-up bunk

chain

24"

³⁄₈" plywood

Built-in bunk with storage boxes underneath. To save space, fold-up bunks can be hung from the wall with chains.

TREE HOUSE ACCESSORIES

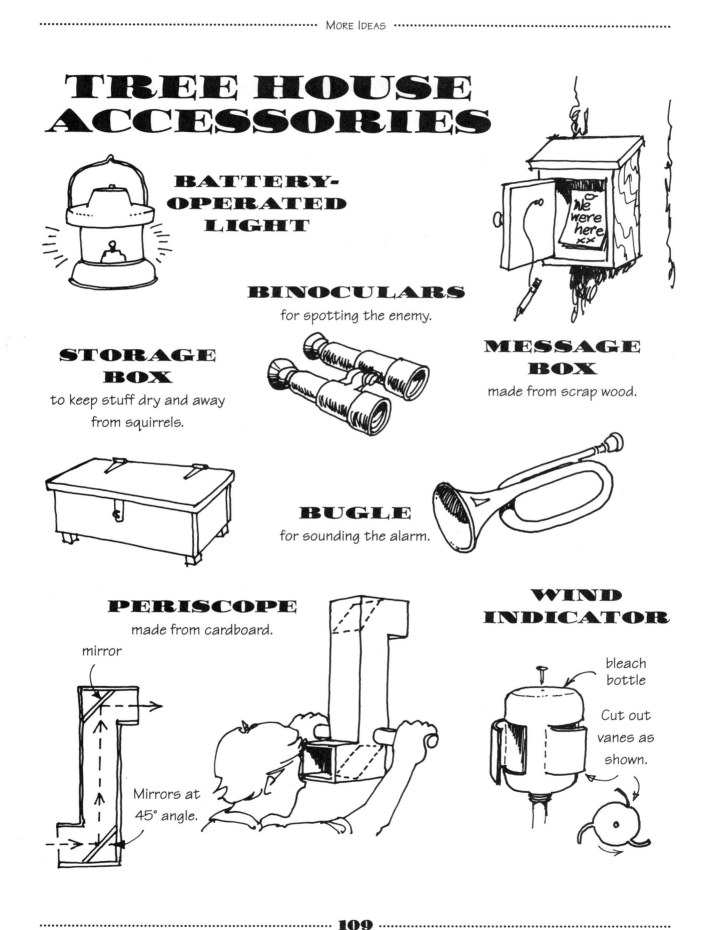

BATTERY-OPERATED LIGHT

BINOCULARS
for spotting the enemy.

We were here xx

STORAGE BOX
to keep stuff dry and away from squirrels.

MESSAGE BOX
made from scrap wood.

BUGLE
for sounding the alarm.

PERISCOPE
made from cardboard.

mirror

Mirrors at 45° angle.

WIND INDICATOR

bleach bottle

Cut out vanes as shown.

PHONES

In our high-tech world of cellular phones, beepers, and pagers, communication has become increasingly important. Tree houses, however, require less elaborate means of calling home. Here are some ways of accomplishing this.

Tie a string from your home to your tree house and attach a bell. When Mom and Dad need to get your attention, they can just pull the string.

For short distances, two tin cans work great. Punch a hole in the bottom of each can . . .

. . . and attach a string, knotting both ends, between the cans.

Notes can be sent in a basket via a trolley made from a clothesline pulley.

PULLEYS

Pulleys are very popular in tree houses and can be especially useful when building the house (see pages 27–28).

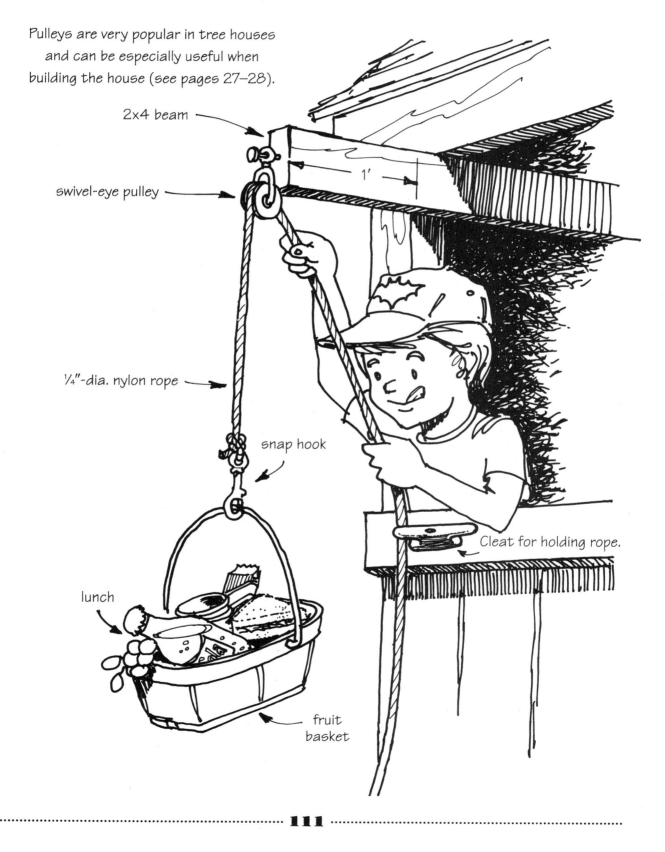

2x4 beam

swivel-eye pulley

1'

¼"-dia. nylon rope

snap hook

Cleat for holding rope.

lunch

fruit basket

TROLLEYS

Overhead cable trolleys have become increasingly popular in recent years.
They can be a lot of fun to ride on, but they must be made SAFE. Here are some tips.

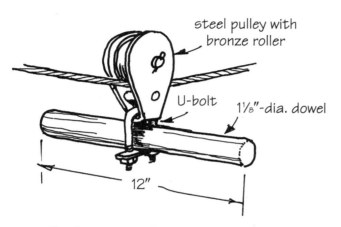

steel pulley with bronze roller

U-bolt

1⅛"-dia. dowel

12"

Two rollers make the trolley less wobbly.

ALTERNATE TROLLEY

Don't try to make a trolley out of a clothesline pulley (the plastic wheel will melt under the friction). Instead, use one or two pulleys supported by a steel cable.

Rig the cable above the launching platform. Allow enough slack in the cable so that the rider will travel uphill at the end of the ride. This will act as a brake. Anchor the cable to a strong side branch, rather than to the tree trunk, to avoid the possibility of running into the tree.

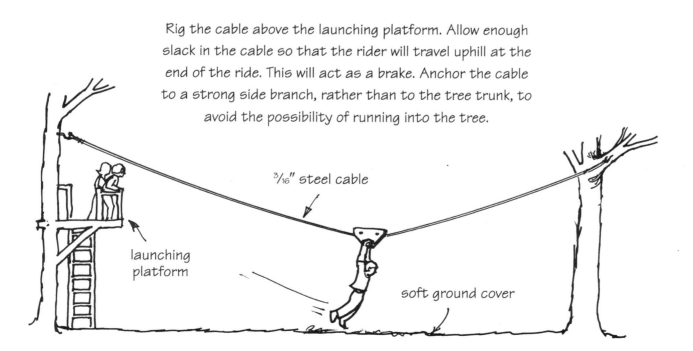

³⁄₁₆" steel cable

launching platform

soft ground cover

HOW TO ATTACH
WIRE CABLE

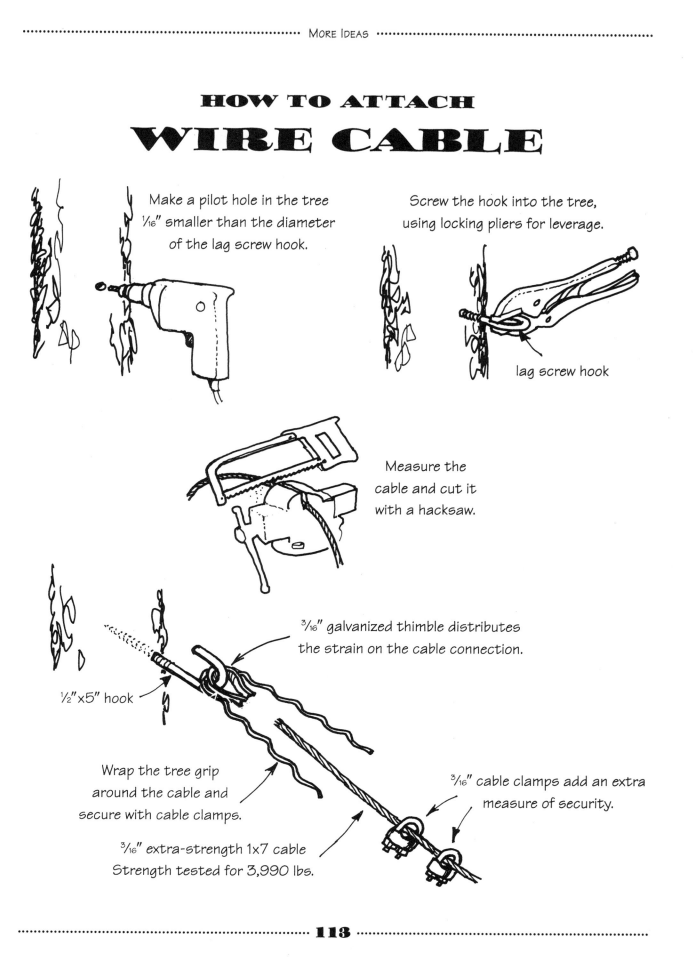

Make a pilot hole in the tree ¹⁄₁₆" smaller than the diameter of the lag screw hook.

Screw the hook into the tree, using locking pliers for leverage.

lag screw hook

Measure the cable and cut it with a hacksaw.

³⁄₁₆" galvanized thimble distributes the strain on the cable connection.

½"x5" hook

Wrap the tree grip around the cable and secure with cable clamps.

³⁄₁₆" cable clamps add an extra measure of security.

³⁄₁₆" extra-strength 1x7 cable Strength tested for 3,990 lbs.

SLIDES

Slides are great fun, as they provide a quick exit from the tree house in case of an emergency. Use ¾"-thick MDO plywood, which is an exterior plywood with a smooth surface and is good to slide on.

Build the slide at a 28° angle for best results.

To protect your hands from splinters, cut an old rubber garden hose lengthwise and nail it to the top edge of the rail.

For added protection, give the slide several coats of exterior polyurethane.

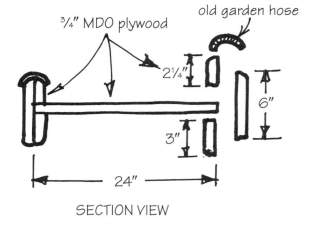

¾" MDO plywood

old garden hose

2¼"

6"

3"

24"

SECTION VIEW

SWINGS

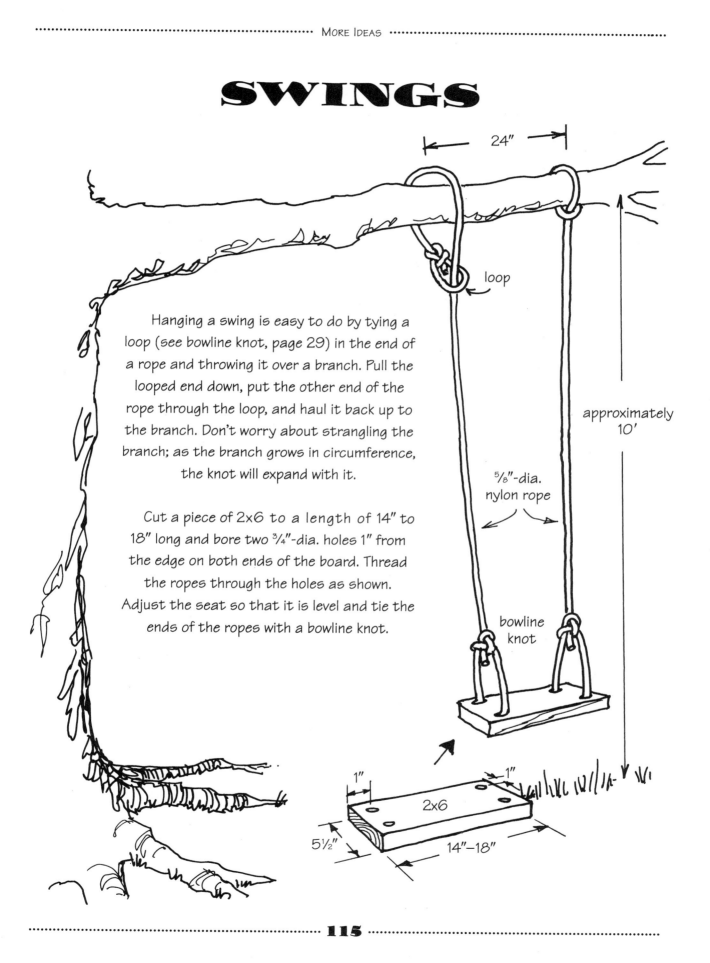

24"

loop

approximately
10'

Hanging a swing is easy to do by tying a
loop (see bowline knot, page 29) in the end of
a rope and throwing it over a branch. Pull the
looped end down, put the other end of the
rope through the loop, and haul it back up to
the branch. Don't worry about strangling the
branch; as the branch grows in circumference,
the knot will expand with it.

Cut a piece of 2x6 to a length of 14" to
18" long and bore two ¾"-dia. holes 1" from
the edge on both ends of the board. Thread
the ropes through the holes as shown.
Adjust the seat so that it is level and tie the
ends of the ropes with a bowline knot.

⅝"-dia.
nylon rope

bowline
knot

1"

1"

2x6

5½"

14"–18"

SWINGS continued

If you don't have a branch at the perfect height, you can attach two beams between two trees to support the swing. Since the trees will move independently of each other, make the connection to one tree permanent and the connection to the other flexible.

Nail together two 2x6 blocks cut to different lengths so that the bottom block fits between the two beams and the top block fits over the beams. Repeat this to make a second set of blocks.

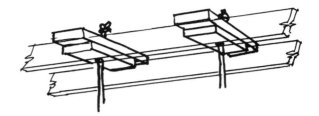

Hang the swing from the center of each block assembly.

HOW HIGH?

When planning your swing, keep in mind that the higher a swing goes, the farther the fall! Short swings seem more age appropriate for young children. It takes more pumps to get a long swing to the top of its arc. The longer the swing, the longer the arc, so make sure there is nothing in front of the swing for the swinger to kick.

TIRE SWINGS

An automobile tire hung vertically from a tree is fun to use. If you suspend it horizontally, however, as shown here, about 18" above the ground, it can swing in three different directions — forward and backward, side to side, and in figure eights!

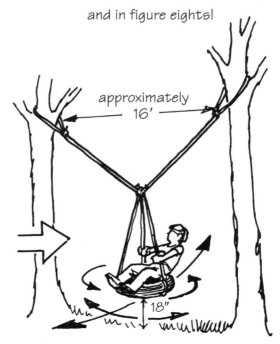

approximately 16'

18"

FLAGS

Make your own.
Any material will do, but nylon will
last longer than many other materials.

Color your own design with
permanent markers.

oval rope hole

bronze
eye snap

reinforced
edge

Make your own
PULLEY.

¼"-dia.
peg

¾"-dia.
dowel in
a ⅞"-dia.
hole.

2"-dia. flagpole

brass
grommet

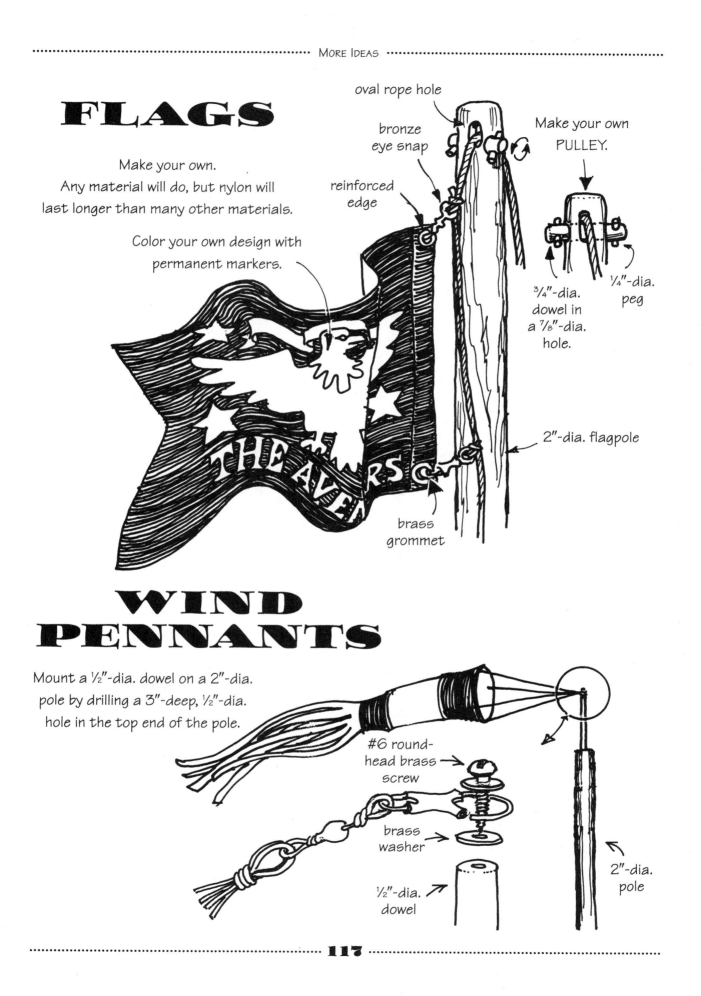

WIND PENNANTS

Mount a ½"-dia. dowel on a 2"-dia.
pole by drilling a 3"-deep, ½"-dia.
hole in the top end of the pole.

#6 round-
head brass
screw

brass
washer

½"-dia.
dowel

2"-dia.
pole

PLAY TREE

If you don't want to build a tree house, here is another way to use a tree.

Keep Out

PLAN YOUR OWN
TREE HOUSE

Place a sheet of tracing paper over this grid and draw a plan (top) view, a front view, and a side view of your tree house. This will help you when picking out your lumber.

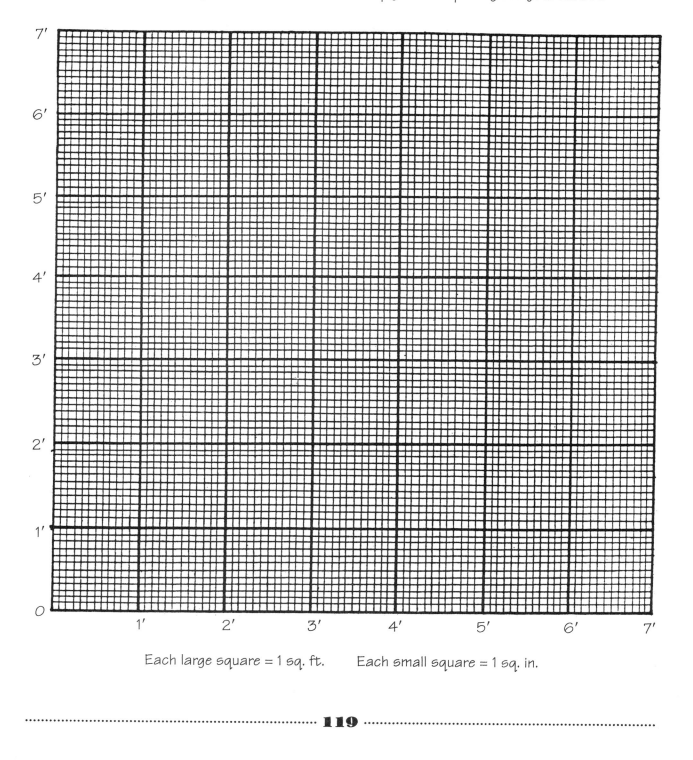

Each large square = 1 sq. ft.   Each small square = 1 sq. in.

PERSPECTIVE DRAWING

Lay a piece of tracing paper over this grid and draw your tree house
in perspective to see how it will look when it is finished.

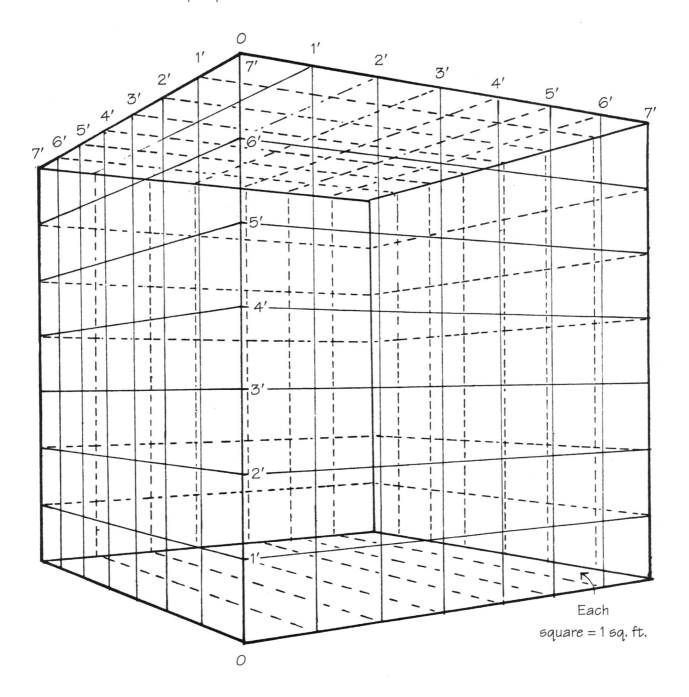

Each
square = 1 sq. ft.

Deed

Whereas these premises have outlived their usefulness, I hereby deed this property to...

Check
One

- ☐ my Little sister
- ☐ my Little brother
- ☐ my Little neighbor
- ☐ any Kid who wants it

_____   _____
Signed   Date

COPY & CUT

Building Permit

Permission is hereby granted to _____ - architect - builder, at the location of _____, to construct, in the best manner possible, this tree house so that it will be both pleasing to the eye and safe to all who occupy its quarters.

signed

_____
Parent

_____
Neighbor

_____
Builder

_____
Date

seal of GOOD TREE HOUSE CONSTRUCTION

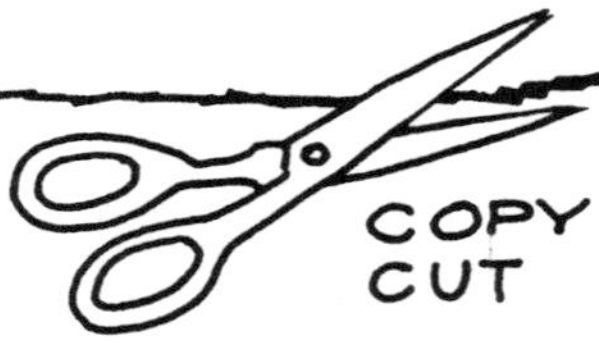

COPY & CUT

the Tree House Club

Be it known that the following persons are tried and trusted members of the Tree House Club:

1. _____ President

2. _____ Vice President

3 _____ Treasurer

4. _____ Secretary of State

5. _____ Secretary of Defense

6. _____ Mascot

COPY & CUT

You're Welcome

Please feel free to use our tree house. We are very proud of it and hope you like it too. Please help Keep it neat and tidy.

_____
owner

COPY & CUT

Tree houses are great for protecting you from bullies,
skunks, ferocious dogs, and creepy crawlies.

Sources

Cable, cable clamps, hooks, tree grips & thimbles

A. M. Leonard (nursery supply house)

241 Fox Drive

P.O. Box 816

Piqua, OH 45356

1-800-543-8955

Hand tools

Harbor Freight Tools (inexpensive mail-order tools)

3491 Mission Oaks Blvd.

Camarillo, CA 93011-6010

1-800-423-2567

Lumber & hardware

Home Depot (check the phone book for the nearest store)

Rope, pulleys & fittings

Defender Industries, Inc. (marine supply house)

42 Great Neck Road

Waterford, CT 06385

1-800-628-8225

About the Authors

Kevin Kwan

DAVID STILES is a designer/builder and illustrator, and the author of eight other how-to books, including *Sheds*. A graduate of Pratt Institute and The Academy of Fine Arts in Florence, Italy, he is the winner of two awards from the New York Planning Commission. His articles have appeared in *House Beautiful, Country Journal, HomeMechanix,* and the *New York Times.*

JEAN TRUSTY STILES, a graduate of Wheaton College, lives in New York City, where she is an actress/model and an instructor of English as a Second Language. Jeanie and David have written *Playhouses You Can Build, Kids' Furniture You Can Build, Garden Projects, Storage Projects,* and *Woodworking Simplified,* and have appeared on numerous television programs, including Lifetime Television and the Discovery Channel's "Home Matters" show. They have a 23-year-old daughter, Lief Anne, who recently graduated from Duke University, and they divide their time between New York City and East Hampton, New York.

Note to Readers

If you build a tree house that you are particularly proud of, we would love to see it. Please send a photo to us: David & Jeanie Stiles, c/o Houghton Mifflin, 222 Berkeley Street, Boston, MA 02116